Equipment Leasing and Financing

Equipment Leasing and Financing

A Product Sales and Business Profit Strategy

Richard M. Contino

BEP BUSINESS EXPERT PRESS

Equipment Leasing and Financing: A Product Sales and Business Profit Strategy

First published in 2020 by
Business Expert Press, LLC
222 East 46th Street, New York, NY 10017
www.businessexpertpress.com

ISBN-13: 978-1-94999-192-5 (paperback)
ISBN-13: 978-1-94999-193-2 (e-book)

Business Expert Press Business Law and Corporate Risk Management Collection

Collection ISSN: 2333-6722 (print)
Collection ISSN: 2333-6730 (electronic)

Cover and interior design by Exeter Premedia Services Private Ltd., Chennai, India

First edition: 2020

10 9 8 7 6 5 4 3 2 1

Printed in the United States of America.

Dedication

Penelope, May-Lynne, and Matthew

Abstract

This book explains how companies that sell equipment and other products can increase product sales and add an additional profit center by establishing their own innovative leasing and financing operation. Industry data shows that the need for equipment and other product financing has evolved over the past few decades to where now nine out of 10 U.S. companies use leasing or other forms of third-party financing to acquire the equipment or other products they need. For market-aggressive companies offering products for sale, having an available in-house customer product leasing and financing program as a product marketing strategy can dramatically increase their ability to close product sales.

In the past, establishing an in-house financing activity was difficult and expensive, requiring unique and substantial additional business operational and financing components in addition to an extensive learning curve. This is no longer the case. In recent years, there have been wide-spread market advances surrounding the financing of equipment and other products that enable forward-thinking companies to cost-effectively establish their own in-house product financing activity, using readily available, state-of the-art financing software programs, and third-party *back-office* services to manage any part of the financing process.

This book will provide a product vendor with the turnkey *know-how* it needs to assess the viability of establishing an in-house equipment financing operation, as well as the various considerations needed to set up and run its own cost-effective and profitable product financing activity.

Keywords

equipment financing; equipment leasing; leasing; financing; product marketing; product sales; product financing; conditional sales agreements; lease agreements; product financing agreements; product sale financing; product sale leasing

Contents

Introduction

This book will address how companies that sell equipment and other products can set up their own innovative leasing and financing operation to increase product sales and add a solid new business profit center. Historically, developing an in-house product vendor financing activity was a major and costly undertaking, but, today, doing so can be readily and cost-effectively done by a product vendor of virtually any size using market available, state-of-the-art software and outsourced services. It is a known fact that product seller customers prefer financing offered by product sellers, believing it will not only be the most favorable financing arrangement available, but will also involve less financing *red tape*. A belief often true.

Industry data shows that the need for equipment and other product financing has evolved over the past few decades to the point where now nine out of 10 U.S. companies use leasing or other forms of third-party financing to acquire the equipment or other products they need. At the time of this writing, the latest available annual business statistics (2017) from the Equipment Leasing and Finance Foundation show that businesses acquired 1.7 trillion U.S. dollars of equipment and software, 60 percent of which, or over one trillion U.S. dollars, was financed through leasing, 48 percent of this total, the most common method; followed by lines of credit, 9 percent of this total, and secured loans, 8 percent of this total. For market-aggressive companies offering products for sale, having an available in-house customer product leasing and financing program can dramatically increase their ability to close product sales.

Virtually, all but a small percentage of product vendors who use financing to support and increase product sales rely on arrangements with third-party independent or bank-affiliated leasing companies to provide customer financing. These third-party arrangements, often provided on a non-disclosed (*private label*) basis under the name, or a name derivation, of the product seller, can be very profitable for the leasing companies. Generally, however, these third-party programs are not as flexible as product vendors need today because of old-style financing documents, transaction structuring, and rigorous credit criteria and because these programs often have processing complexities.

A relative few innovative companies, such as Cisco Systems Inc., do not generally rely on third-party leasing companies and banks for their customer product financing, but instead have developed their own internal and profitable customer product finance function. These few companies derive not only profits from their product sales, but also from financing charges and product re-sales at the end of any lease term. In the case of Cisco System Capital Corporation, the product financing arm of Cisco Systems Inc., the setting up and running of a financing activity when it did, in the late 1980s, and for which the author provided consulting services, required not only extensive groundbreaking approaches, but also involved a considerable startup effort and expense commitment, as well as a steep learning curve. However, companies that have established their own financing activity, like Cisco, have benefited from a powerful product marketing tool—the immediate ability to offer turnkey product financing at the time of a proposed product sale, giving them a distinct competitive marketing edge and the ability to close sales quickly.

Unfortunately, even with the clear evolving financing needs of product customers, most product vendors suffer from *old-style thinking*, refusing to consider establishing their own financing operation, claiming that it would not be part of their core business activity. These companies overlook the fact that an in-house product financing activity that is tailored to fit customer product acquisition needs should simply be considered a way to refine and enhance their existing product marketing activity, a critical component of any product vendor's business operation. In the past, their reluctance was often well founded, in part because of the difficulty and expense of establishing a financing activity, which required unique and substantial additional business operational and financing components in addition to an extensive learning curve. This is no longer the case. In recent years, there have been widespread market advances surrounding the financing of equipment and other products that enable forward-thinking companies to cost-effectively establish their own in-house product financing activity, using readily available, state-of-the-art financing software programs that can, for example, fully automate the processing and evaluation of customer creditworthiness and the issuance of financing proposals and financing documents, all online. Couple that with readily available third-party *back-office* services to manage any part of the financing process, such as payment billing and collection, and the setting up of a cost-effective and fully operational tailored turnkey product financing activity is now a very manageable possibility.

This book will provide a product vendor with the turnkey *know-how* they need to assess the viability of establishing an in-house equipment financing operation, as well as the various considerations needed to set up and run their own cost-effective and profitable product financing activity.

CHAPTER 1

Product Leasing and Financing: A Marketing Strategy for Product Sellers

Product Financing: A Critical Element of Product Sales

The financing of equipment in the United States, based on the most recently available market data, exceeds 1 trillion U.S. dollars a year. With this type of market acceptance, there is no doubt that a product vendor having customer equipment and other product financing readily available can be a critical component in securing a product sale. This is particularly true if the financing does not involve much, if any, *red tape*, is offered in easy-to-understand terms and meets a customer's tax, accounting, and legal needs.

A Basic Overview of Equipment and Product Financing

Leasing, a Simple Concept

The leasing of equipment is a well-accepted way for businesses to acquire their needed equipment. A lease is simply a contract where the owner of equipment, the lessor, agrees to let a company in need of the equipment, the lessee, use the equipment for an agreed-upon period, the lease term, and lease payment. At the end of the lease term, the lessee returns the equipment to the lessor. The concept is simple; the lease documents, however, can often be complex and need to be carefully drafted, but once settled on, they require little, if any, re-visiting. The lease document is discussed in greater detail in Chapter 9.

Alternative Financing Structures

In addition to the financing of equipment under a lease arrangement, there are other equipment and product financing arrangements that allow businesses to acquire their needed equipment or other products without having to pay the full product purchase price up-front, discussed in greater detail in Chapter 9. For example, a product acquisition can be financed using a conditional sale arrangement, essentially a form of debt financing, where the product user pays a specific periodic payment, such as monthly, over the financing term, and at the end of the financing term, owns the product free and clear. Interestingly, a conditional sale financing can be set up using a lease agreement by simply giving the lessee the option to purchase the product at the end of the lease term for 1 U.S. dollar. Another example would be when product financing is arranged through what are referred to as managed services or fee-per-use agreements, also discussed in Chapter 9, where equipment along with related services, such as maintenance or repair services, or supplies, such as disposables used with the equipment, are provided for an agreed-upon term and periodic payment.

Offering Financing as a Key In-House Product Marketing Strategy

In-House Financing Can Sell Your Products

In today's market, product users are looking for favorable, cost-effective ways to finance their needed equipment and other product acquisitions. They often favor financing offered by product vendors, feeling that the arrangements will be on better terms than can be obtained from their banks or from independent leasing or financing companies, and, generally, they are correct. Clearly, product vendors with readily available in-house financing for products they sell have a distinct marketing advantage over competitors who do not have readily available financing to offer during their product sales process.

Cost-Effective Market Innovations Create New Profit Center Opportunities

Currently, the greater percentage of product financing is provided by independent (third party) leasing and financing companies or banks with equipment financing affiliates because of the various highly specialized components needed in a financing activity, such as credit assessment, documentation and deal processing, and financing management. Accordingly, companies that considered setting up an *in-house* product financing operation in the past were generally well advised to rely on outside financing sources because of the specialized operational components needed for an effective financing activity. Notwithstanding the operational and expertise challenges and added cost of running a financing company, however, a few product vendors, such as Cisco Systems, Inc., benefited greatly in increased product sales from the setup of their own in-house financing activity.

In today's market, the availability of emerging technology products and services tailored toward a financing operation have substantially reduced the cost and challenge of setting up and running an in-house product financing operation. For the informed product vendor, therefore, setting up and running an in-house financing operation is now a viable option. There are now service and product providers who offer virtually all the components necessary to establish a financing activity, giving product vendors a cost-effective option to set up and run an in-house product activity that adds a new and effective marketing component for product sales. Because of the relatively recent innovative product offerings, which include specialized financing-related software, and the availability of third-party service providers offering specific solutions for a financing operation, product vendors should now re-visit the setup of an in-house financing activity because having an efficient, user-friendly, and cost-effective product financing readily available will not only enhance and increase product sales but can also add a substantial new business profit component. For example, companies like Terra Vista Software (https://terravistasoftware.com), based in Orinda, California, have developed software tools that can be used to process and manage a product financing activity, online. The Terra Vista software can automatically process a customer's credit application, price optional financing offers, deliver a customer proposal, and if a proposal is accepted by the customer, set up and deliver the financing documentation, all easily managed by the software licensee. That coupled with many qualified *back-office* service providers who can handle the billing and collection of financing payments and assess applicable state and local taxes due and payable, minimizes the *expertise* a product vendor needs to set up an effective and profitable financing activity as a part of its product marketing strategy. Accordingly, using service and technology product providers offering all the essential components necessary to set up and efficiently run a financing activity, product vendors now have the opportunity, in addition to adding a new and effective marketing component for product sales, to create a new profit center.

Product Vendor Financing Using Third-Party Financing Companies or Banks: The Traditional Approach

The Third-Party Leasing and Financing Market

Independent and bank-affiliated leasing companies have, over many decades, provided a valuable financing service for product vendors by offering a variety of equipment and other product financing alternatives for product vendor customers. Most of these financing companies are well run and offer very effective and attractive financing programs for product vendors to make available to their customers, with some, often non-bank-affiliated, willing to take greater credit risks than others are comfortable doing for reasons discussed later in this book.

How Leasing and Financing Companies Develop Product Vendor Business

In the early years of the leasing and financing business, most independent and bank-affiliated leasing and financing companies approached potential product users directly with their own sales personnel, rather than working with product vendors, to find financing opportunities, an effort that required a significant sales staff and a time-consuming effort.

Today, however, leasing and financing companies understand the benefit of affiliating with a product vendor and taking advantage of a vendor sales force to identify financing opportunities, setting up with product vendors what are referred to as *vendor programs*. Under a third-party vendor program, discussed in greater detail in Chapter 3, the financing company contractually agrees with a product vendor to offer financing to interested product vendor customers.

The fact is that having available product financing offered at the inception of the product sales process has become so beneficial to the product sales process that leasing and financing companies offering *vendor* financing programs specifically for customers of product vendors have developed a major and lucrative leasing and financing business segment. Prior to the emergence of the vendor program concept, third-party leasing and financing companies simply looked for product users who wanted financing for their product acquisitions. By working with a product vendor, a financing company can piggyback on the efforts of a vendor's product sales personnel, a far more efficient and cost-effective way to identify potential financing customers. Over the years, the financing companies with aggressive and effective vendor financing program strategies have been able to substantially increase financing sales, and product vendors are now an aggressively sought-after market opportunity by many financing companies. As a result, vendor programs are now a major profit center for many third-party financing companies.

Third-Party Product Vendor Financing Structures Offered Today

Generally, the financing offered by third-party leasing and financing companies to product vendors for their customers consists of equipment leases and conditional sales arrangements, which are both effective and have, in the past, satisfied the needs of most product vendor customers. However, because of the relatively recent changes in the accounting rules, the traditionally offered financing structures can be somewhat limiting and, thus, often do not fully facilitate or support a product vendor's sales or business needs or the needs of their customers. For example, traditional long-term finance leases, discussed in Chapter 8, now must be reported on the lessee's financial statements as long-term debt obligations, something that had not previously been the case. Additionally, product vendors are increasingly offering services or supplies along with equipment or other products they sell to augment profits, which they want financed as a package. These types of contract offerings, often in a form referred to as managed services or fee-per-use agreements, are drafted by product vendors and provide equipment and services as a *bundled* offering, at times on a charge-per-use basis. Unfortunately, for product vendors offering *bundled* equipment, services and/or supplies, many financing companies, particularly the more traditional ones, have either refused or been slow to evolve in the marketplace, to accommodate financing for these types of agreements. The result has been to substantially limit or eliminate a product vendor's new product sale strategies.

The Pros and Cons for a Product Vendor in Using Third-Party Leasing and Financing Companies

Working with an independent or bank-affiliated leasing and financing company has many benefits for a product vendor. The vendor gets immediate access to state-of-the-art customer product financial structuring, competitive lease and financing rates, acceptable lease and financing documents, guidance on current federal and state tax, as well as the new financing accounting, rules and access to an effective and often quick financing process. As a result, a knowledgeable and experienced independent leasing and financing company can significantly augment a product vendor's product sales process, thus assisting in and increasing product sales.

At times, there can be distinct disadvantages in working with third-party leasing and financing companies. First and foremost, a very few are not as reputable as they should be, stating an ability to provide aggressive financing or what appears to be a customer-friendly financing process that, in fact, will not be followed through once the product vendor agrees to a vendor program. Some have overly aggressive collection personnel who can damage the product vendor's customer relationship through their vendor affiliation, particularity if the financing program is done under the product vendor's name, referred to as a *private label* program, where the customer is made to believe that the product financing is being offered and done by the product vendor, with all documents and marketing material, and even phone calls and e-mails, issued under the product vendor's name. Making matters even more challenging in using third-party financing companies is the fact that a few insert fine-print deceptive, or *gotcha*, provisions in their financing documents, such as onerous lease renewal provisions that automatically extend the financing term for long periods if the lessee fails to notify the lessor within a very small timeframe of its desire to return the equipment at lease end. This then disrupts the customer relationship. And, finally, some have distinct limitations on the type of customer contracts they will provide financing for, such as not offering financing for bundled equipment and services contracts or contracts that charge based on product use. The result is that a product vendor often does not have available customer financing that fits its market needs and sales strategies in the current highly competitive marketplace.

Advantages of an In-House Product Financing Operation

There are a number of obvious advantages for a product vendor in offering in-house financing in connection with its product sales activity and a few less obvious ones.

Facilitates Product Sales

As already mentioned, product financing facilitates product sales by providing an easy way for the product user to acquire products he or she needs. Providing a prospective customer with not only a product offering, but also a simple and quick way to finance the product's acquisition is an obvious sales advantage and historically has been known to increase product sales.

Faster Product Sale Closings

Offering readily available product financing at the time of a proposed product sale, giving a customer the option to simply sign a lease document that provides equipment or other products, can shorten the sales process. Doing so, for example, can eliminate a customer's need to review available cash or bank lines of credit for a product acquisition, making the acquisition decision easier and faster.

Control over the Product Aftermarket Protects New Product Sales

The effect of a secondary (used equipment) market for products financed by third-party leasing companies is something often overlooked by a product vendor. Typically, as you will learn in Chapter 2, a leasing company makes its money primarily from its interest rate spread over its cost of money and operations and then, looks to generating substantial profits from end-of-lease product re-leasing or sales, referred to as *residual* profits. As most leasing companies have relatively small equipment re-marketing departments, they typically *dump* end-of-lease equipment quickly into the market, often through equipment brokers. This type of used *aftermarket* equipment *fire sale* can dramatically and adversely affect new product sales, particularly for products with a long useful life. But, by controlling the aftermarket sales through their own in-house financing operation, a product vendor can not only protect their new product sales, but they can generate additional profits from the secondary market activity. For those product vendors who decide to set up a product financing activity using a third-party financing company vendor program, discussed in Chapter 3, rather than setting up an in-house financing operation, they can achieve at least partial control over any aftermarket product risks by having a product re-marketing agreement with the third-party financing company that allows them to manage, to a greater extent, the sale of their equipment in the secondary market.

Can Dramatically Increase Business Profits

As also already suggested, leasing and financing profits can add to profits from product sales, sometimes dramatically.

Opens the Door to Collateral Services Sales and Repeat Business

Its a well-known sales fact that once a company has developed a customer relationship, such as through a long-term and ongoing product sales or an equipment financing relationship, the customer rapport established can ease discussions and facilitate new and repeat business collateral to the actual product sale, including the sales of additional products, services, and supplies. For example, many customers take time to thoroughly initially review and negotiate a lease contract, but when the document has been agreed to, they are often comfortable using the same document for new transactions without further review, minimizing legal and other document review time and costs. Accordingly, having a lease document in place with a product customer can provide an advantage over a product competitor that introduces new financing documentation that needs time-consuming legal review.

Document Control

One of the biggest challenges historically for equipment financing has been financing documentation complexity. Unfortunately, many third-party financing companies, for example, use financing contracts drafted in a way that makes it difficult for business people to understand, and that sometimes imposes onerous conditions. This is slowly changing because of product vendor customer needs and market competition, but something that a product vendor with their own in-house financing operation would have more control over. While it is necessary, for example, for a financing contract to be drafted in a way that ensures the customer payment and other obligations can be enforced, the terms provided by third-party financing companies are often overkill. For a product vendor to develop more marketing-oriented financing documents, however, they must understand the basic contract foundation objectives, discussed in Chapter 9, and work with experienced legal counsel to develop product financing documents that are not only effective from a legal and business standpoint but easy for its customer to review and accept.

Disadvantages of an In-House Financing Operation

While there are many advantages to an in-house product financing operation, there are some distinct challenges, which, with the right strategy, are manageable.

Credit Risks

Clearly, providing in-house financing for a customer exposes the product vendor to customer credit risk. Making a credit assessment takes a particular expertise, but today, readily available software from companies, such as PayNet (https://paynet.com), can dramatically reduce the credit assessment risks, drawing on a wealth of customer historical data and existing and historical market trends, to benchmark, online, where there may be an undue credit risk. Hiring an experienced credit manager, however, is an essential part of any financing activity to reduce and manage customer credit risks.

Product Re-Marketing Risks

Getting used equipment back at the end of a lease term or earlier because, for example, of a financing contract default, can jeopardize financing profits, particularly if the product drops significantly in value in the used marketplace and the product vendor was anticipating, as part of its financing profit, proceeds from the sale or re-lease of the product or as collateral to offset any customer credit risk for any shortfall resulting from a contract payment default. In this situation, product vendors with their inherent product knowledge, particularly if they have product refurbishment capabilities and existing customer base contacts, can offset this risk through secondary market product marketing, something independent leasing companies without similar capabilities can rarely do.

Summary

The establishment of an in-house leasing activity by a product vendor can not only increase product sales, but can also add a new profit center, something that historically has been difficult and expensive to do, but today, it is something that should now be a viable consideration for any aggressive product vendor.

CHAPTER 2

The Business of Leasing and Financing Equipment

Overview

In connection with making a determination of whether to set up an in-house product vendor financing operation, it is essential to have a general understanding of how the equipment financing business operates in the United States. Many of the concepts used in the United States have parallels to how financing works overseas as well. The information in this chapter is designed to provide an overview of the key business elements, using as a base the leasing of equipment.

Why Would a Company Enter the Equipment Financing Business?

The equipment financing business in the United States is mature, and the competition is intense, and, accordingly, the traditional equipment financing business may not have the most potential for a straight investor. But, for product vendors, the story is different, with many unique and attractive profit opportunities available if the financing activity is approached knowledgeably and systematically. If it is not, mistakes are inevitable and substantial losses are likely, something attested to over and over during the past decades by the many nonbank, and bank-affiliated, leasing company problems, closings, sell-offs, and bankruptcies from a variety of historically repetitive and obvious mistakes. Mistakes often result from top management's lack of streetwise business and operational expertise, shortsighted attempts to maintain near-term profits, risky product financings, or the desire to increase profit-based bonuses. So, for a product vendor considering setting up an in-house leasing and financing business to expand and support product sales, and add a substantial new profit center, a solid understanding of basic business strategies that successful leasing companies use today to survive and make money is important.

The threshold question is why would a product vendor set up a leasing or financing operation? There are a number of basic reasons already mentioned, with the key reason being the ability to facilitate the sale of its products. Paying 200 U.S. dollars a month for five years, rather than 10,000 U.S. dollars upfront, for needed equipment makes the customer's product purchase decision much easier. Another key consideration is to control to some extent the secondary (used) equipment market, thereby protecting new product sales prices by not having third-party financing companies dump used products in the market at low prices, as well as to derive profits from the sale or re-leasing of used products that come off lease.

What Are the Particular Challenges for a Product Vendor?

A major challenge for any product vendor considering the establishment of an in-house product financing operation is overcoming any potential senior management's resistance to setting up an operation not considered a *core* business activity. Unfortunately, this type of *old-school* thinking overlooks a viable new product marketing strategy, now possible because of the many available state-of-the-art software products and third-party services that can be used to implement a cost-effective and manageable product financing activity. Of course, in addition to having available money to invest in financing transactions, a product vendor must be prepared to allocate some basic funds to the setup of the financing operation, which, at a minimum, would include the cost of hiring a credit manager and an operational person to ensure all aspects are correctly implemented, as well as the cost of acquiring applicable software for processing and managing the financing activity and developing contract documentation and, possibly, contracting with a qualified *back-office* service provider to handle billing, collection, and portfolio report generation, all discussed in Chapter 4.

Key Traditional Profit Strategies to Consider

As stated earlier, for a product vendor to properly evaluate starting an in-house financing activity, a basic understanding of how leasing companies generally make money is essential. Aside from financing profits, there can be other profit areas, many of which are not obvious to the lay person.

Valuable Assets Acquired with Customer Money

In very simple, everyday terms, how would you react if a wealthy neighbor asked you to lease her an 80,000 U.S. dollar BMW for her business use? Assume you could borrow the entire purchase price from your local bank at a rate that gave you a 200 U.S. dollar monthly profit. And, assume the loan could be based solely on your neighbor's credit, having no impact on your future borrowing capabilities. Further, if your neighbor defaulted on her lease payments for any reason, you would not be responsible to pay off any remaining loan balance. Assume also that the lease would be for seven years, the rents would pay off the entire bank loan and, when the lease ended, your neighbor would have to return the car to you in excellent condition. The result: at the end of seven years, you would own what could be a cream-puff BMW, free, and clear, to do with as you wish. Sell it. Re-lease it. Or, simply use it as your personal car. Sounds good? Most people would agree that it does. That is the basic business of equipment leasing in a nutshell.

You might think it is not possible to get a bank to loan what might be your now fledging company money to finance a customer's product needs without holding your company responsible for its repayment. But, assuming your company meets a lender's minimum credit standards, so-called nonrecourse equipment loans are available because banks and other lenders will loan money on the strength of a strong lease contract with a good credit lessee, without relying on the creditworthiness of the owner-lessor. As you will see in Chapter 9, your lease must be what is referred to as a net finance lease and contain what is referred to as a hell or high water payment clause, obligating the lessee to keep making the rent payments no matter what happens, even if the equipment is destroyed or otherwise unavailable for use. So, if you have a hell or high water, net finance lease with a good credit lessee, nonrecourse equipment loans are available.

The most interesting aspect of nonrecourse loans based on equipment leases is they, in effect, provide the lessor (the equipment-owner) with an unlimited borrowing capacity and no loan repayment obligation if the lessee defaults. The exact same result would be true if the BMW was financed with a conditional sale or other type of correctly drafted financing contract.

Now, let us take this hypothetical example a step further. What if 10 individuals asked you to lease them BMWs under the same terms that also provided you with a 200 U.S. dollars per month profit on each car? Your profit would be 2,000 U.S. dollars a month and you would own 10 BMWs at the end of their respective seven-year lease terms, all free and clear. Not a bad return for a no-money-down investment, particularly if you could borrow the entire cost of the BMWs from your bank, something that is possible with a correctly written lease contract.

While this over-simplified hypothetical may not be realistic in the automobile financing market, an extremely competitive market where finance companies have to maintain an equity, or end-of-lease *residual*, investment in a car making it unlikely that you as suggested in the hypothetical could borrow the entire cost of a BMW from a bank, it does put into quick perspective one basic strategy used in the leasing business-getting credit-worthy companies to pay for, and maintain, assets that can be sold or re-released at the end of the financing term for additional profit, all the time making a profit while waiting for their return. All the leasing company must do, once a lease deal is put in place, is to send out the rent bill and deposit the payment checks when they come in.

Windfall Profits: A Possibility

Now let us assume in the prior section example that, at the end of the seven-year lease, each BMW was worth 25% of the original cost, and the rents paid off the entire borrowed BMW purchase cost. In addition to a 200 U.S. dollar monthly profit, selling each car at the end of lease would bring in 20,000 U.S. dollars in end-of-lease, or residual value, revenues.

The residual value revenue expectations, what assets are expected to be worth at the end of their lease periods, are an important part of today's leasing business. It is not unusual for equipment residual values to range from 10 to 100% of the equipment's original cost, and sometimes even higher. The residual values, of course, depend on the type of asset, its return condition, its useful life, inflation, and market demand. For example, in the past, some 10-year-old river barges sold for prices in excess of their original purchase price.

In the early years of the leasing business, when competition was not intense and lessee customers were less sophisticated, financing rates (and financing profits) were high; what an asset was expected to be worth at the end of its lease term was almost irrelevant. A lessor had made all the money it needed from the lease transaction, even if the asset had to be junked. But, as time went on, many leasing companies quickly found there was a lot of added profit potential in the sales and re-leasing of assets that came off lease. In fact, in the early years of the leasing business, many aircraft lessors made lottery-like windfall profits from selling off their end-of-lease aircraft, with some aircraft end-of-lease sale values approaching, or exceeding, the original cost. Add to that the fact that these aircraft lessors had returned, through lease term rents, all but a minimal amount (often between 10 and 15% of the original cost) of their invested principal, and made a tidy profit, and you had some very happy aircraft lessors. The same became true for lessors of other long-life assets. As you might expect, all leasing companies soon caught on to the aircraft and barge residual *end game* and began to stay alert for high residual return possibilities in other types of equipment as well. In fact, equipment residuals became such a major profit component that some lessors even adopted a strategy of acquiring multi-million-dollar high residual value potential equipment solely for the end-of-lease sale or re-lease profits. They cut their lease term profits to the bare minimum necessary to win business, with rents often covering little more than the basic transaction cost of money and overhead costs, anticipating substantial profits when the equipment came off lease. In fact, some leasing companies became so aggressive that they wrote leases that produced a loss during the lease term, counting on the possibility that after the initial lease term ended, the cash flow squeeze was over and yearly residual profits would provide solid bottom-line returns. Heavy reliance on residual profits is still one of the primary profit objectives in leasing today, particularly in *big ticket* leases of long-life assets.

There is risk, however, in placing a primary emphasis on residual profit expectations. Lessors that do incur the possibility that the equipment at lease end will not be worth much more than scrap value if there is no market demand for it or it becomes technologically obsolete. If rents just pay overhead, the potential for loss is great, particularly if unexpected costs are incurred. And, if residual revenue expectations are not met, there is little, or no, economic return for the effort. Some aircraft lessors, for instance, encountering a used aircraft market demand lull in the 1980s, had to store their off-lease aircraft and wait for years for better sale or re-leasing opportunities. Today, equipment and customer industry diversification is used by lessors to reduce this type of risk.

For a product vendor, with an ability to refurbish used equipment, actively managing its end-of-lease re-leases and sales should be a key profit strategy in setting up an in-house financing operation.

The Customer Business Annuity

Developing an extensive customer lease and financing portfolio base should be a strategic business objective of every product vendor, something third-party leasing companies learned early in the leasing business. Qualified prospects are valuable; customers who lease or finance often lease or finance equipment again, at times not even getting competitive bids. And, non-competitive bid situations can assure product vendors of solid economic returns.

Additionally, with qualified leasing customer contacts, a product vendor financing operation has the increased possibility of readily originating new business with little expense, often a simple letter offering new products and lease financing, with a follow-up telephone call, is enough to identify upcoming financing and product sales opportunities. Doing business with a good-paying existing customer has far less credit risk than dealing with a new, unknown customer. No matter how extensive credit due diligence is, it may not uncover credit potholes—financial statements and discussions with trade references and lenders, for example, rarely always tell the whole credit story. Clearly, there is no substitute for first-hand payment experience.

The Low Rate Strategy of Buying Repeat Customers

As suggested earlier, approaching customers who you have already done financing business with makes the product offering and its financing much easier, something third-party leasing companies are well aware of. If rapport and trust have been established through earlier transactions, many of the sales barriers are removed. So, it is often worth considering, when approaching customer prospects, to make your first financing offer very attractive, even at times to consider offering a deal at breakeven financing rates if necessary to win business and, in effect, make an investment in a potentially profitable long-term customer relationship. Satisfied customers often give companies with existing financing relationships exclusive deals, deals that can provide solid profits.

The Master Contract Strategy of Tying Up Repeat Customers

When dealing with new financing customers, third-party leasing companies have learned that putting a master lease or financing agreement in place pays dividends. Under a master financing arrangement, a customer can finance the acquisition of needed products through a simple addendum, cutting financing time and costs for all parties. As explained in Chapter 9, a master lease or master financing contract is a two-part document—the boilerplate portion containing the basic lease or other financing terms and conditions, which will remain the same from deal to deal, and an attachment, often called a schedule, which is a short (typically one to two pages in length) document that permits future business to be simply added by specifically incorporating the new product and financing payment terms under the provisions of the existing master, or boilerplate, document portion. Having only to review a one- or two-page document for lease or other financing deals allows future financings to be handled with minimal effort and expense on both sides. Financing companies with master financing contracts in place are often given preference over competitors that do not because of the ease of documentation, in many situations, getting the last opportunity to win the business by matching the lowest bidder. In fact, in some cases, customers select an incumbent financing company even when it is not the lowest rate or best product price simply because the documentation does not need to be reviewed, making the documentation easy and the document review cost low.

Making Money in the Financing Business

There are many ways to profit in a lease or other financing transaction, some of which have already been suggested. To succeed, and sometimes even survive, in the highly competitive business of equipment financing, a product vendor with an in-house leasing and financing operation should take advantage of every possible profit opportunity used by third-party leasing companies. The obvious areas for leasing profits are tax benefits and, as suggested earlier, interest charges and equipment or product sales or re-leases. The less obvious ones are interim rent charges, penalties for early prepayment, casualty occurrence payments, insurance cost markups, product upgrade financing charges, documentation fees, filing fees, maintenance charges, repair costs, excess use charges, late payment and other collection charges, and equipment re-delivery charges. The same is true for non-lease, or loan, financing, but the financing company does not have available the equipment ownership tax benefits and end-of-financing term re-sale or re-lease profit components.

The intent of the following discussion of leasing and financing profit areas is to enable a product vendor interested in assessing the setup of an equipment financing profit center to have all key aspects pulled together for review.

The Basic Financing Profit Areas

The principal lease transaction profit areas are interest charges, equipment tax benefits, and end-of-lease product re-leasing or re-sale (residual) earnings. Not maximizing any one can significantly reduce the potential for transaction profits. As stated earlier, for a conditional sale or other loan-type financing, a financing operation would not have available any equipment tax benefits or end-of-contract equipment residual earnings.

Interest Charges

The most obvious way to make money in an equipment financing transaction is through financing profits. Financing profit, sometimes referred to as financing spread, is the difference between a financing company's cost of money and its overhead and the lease or other financing interest rate charged. The higher the interest rate charged, the greater the financing profit. For example, assume a lessor set its base cost rate at 9% per annum, which includes its cost of funds, and its allocated overhead, and charges a lease interest rate of 11%. Its financing spread is 2% per annum. By increasing the lease interest rate to 12%, its financing profit increases to 3%.

Market competition, reasonableness and, sometimes, state usury laws, even for commercial customers, limit how much financing spread a financing company can build into its lease or financing rate. Typically, the smaller the equipment lease or financing dollar size, the higher the financing interest rate that can be charged, with customers often looking only to the monthly payment amount, not the implicit financing, or interest, rate charged. For example, lease rates on 5,000 to 50,000 U.S. dollar equipment transactions at the time of this writing can typically range from 10 to 24% per annum, depending on the financing term and dollar amount involved. As transactions approach 100,000 U.S. dollars and over, financing rates move lower, generally in the 5 to 9%+ range. Once the deal size hits 1,000,000 U.S. dollars, apparent lease rates can run 2 to 4% below the lessee's equivalent long-term borrowing rate. In the latter case, for example, a 4,000,000 U.S. dollars, 12-year aircraft lease for a lessee that borrows long-term money at 6% per annum could run anywhere from 1 to 4% per annum, or even less, depending on the equipment ownership tax benefits available and the end-of-lease residual value assumed (invested) by the leasing company. And, if a product vendor has the product sales profit to work with, the apparent lease rate can approach zero or even less, depending on deal structuring. A good example is in automobile leasing, where "0" percent financing is often offered, with the financing company affiliated with or owned by the car manufacturer looking to the car sales price profit to in effect subsidize an apparent low lease rate charge.

Equipment Tax Benefits

The tax aspects of equipment leasing are explained in detail in Chapters 11 and 12. Very often, particularly in multi-million-dollar equipment leases, the tax benefits available to a lessor are a substantial component in computing anticipated transaction investment return, particularly when investment tax credits are available. In fact, potential lessees with excellent credit considering multi-million-dollar lease transactions typically demand that lease rates reflect, and therefore pass through to them in the form of relatively lower rent charges, at least a major portion of transaction tax benefits. Determining how to effectively take into account the transaction tax benefits is complex, but, fortunately today, there are many lessor profit (sometimes referred to as *yield*) analysis software programs, which make the job considerably much easier. One such widely used program, SuperTRUMP, is offered by Ivory Consulting Corporation of Walnut Creek, California (https://ivorycc.com/). The reader is referred to Chapter 7 for a discussion of the lessor yield analysis approach.

As indicated earlier, in the case of a lease transaction, the lessor, as equipment owner, has the right to claim the equipment ownership tax benefits, such as depreciation and any available investment tax credit. In addition, in the case of a leveraged lease transaction, the equipment cost of which is financed in part using third-party debt, there is another tax write-off available, the interest charges on the long-term equipment loan. For a product vendor transferring equipment to an in-house leasing affiliate, determining what tax benefits, and the equipment's tax basis (the equipment dollar amount to which tax benefits can be applied) that can be taken into account for tax purposes, will need to be addressed specifically for each contemplated transaction, a determination to be made by the company's accountants or tax advisors. In a lease situation, the lessee cannot claim for tax purposes any equipment ownership tax benefits. It can, however, deduct the rent payments as a business expense. In the case of an equipment conditional sale arrangement, only the equipment user is entitled to claim the equipment ownership tax benefits.

End-of-Term Equipment Residual Earnings

In pricing a lease transaction (setting the lease rents), a lessor's ideal objective is to have sufficient lease term rents to return its entire equity investment, repay any equipment loans it has used to finance some of the equipment cost, and provide a solid profit, with any end-of-lease equipment sale or re-lease (*residual*) earnings simply as windfall profits. In other words, setting the lessee lease rents using a zero-equipment residual value assumption. In small ticket equipment transactions, this is typically possible. In multi-million-dollar equipment lease transaction, largely due to market competition, this is typically not possible.

Additional Areas of Potential Lease Profit

A leasing and financing company can also add to its leasing and financing profits from less obvious transaction aspects, aforementioned, which include the interim rent or financing charges, prepayment penalties, casualty occurrences, insurance cost markups, upgrade financing costs, documentation fees, filing fees, maintenance charges, repair costs, late payment charges, collection charges, deal re-write charges, and, in the case of a lease, excess use charges, re-marketing fees, and equipment re-delivery charges. Paying attention to each potential profit area can produce attractive additional economic returns.

Interim Lease Rent

One way many lessors build in extra profits is providing for interim rent. Also called pre-commencement, or stub period, rent, it is rent that is payable for a period running from the start of the lease to the beginning of its primary, or main, term. For example, a seven-year lease transaction might provide for the primary term to begin on the first day of the month. If the equipment is not delivered and accepted under the lease contract on the first day of a month, there will be an interim rent period running from the day it was accepted for lease to the first day of the following month. If equipment was delivered, for instance, on the 7th of January, the seven-year period would begin from February 1st, with an interim term running from January 7 through January 31. If the lease rents are computed based on the primary term rents, the stub period rent, typically a pro rata portion of the primary term rents, is a windfall profit. Although not typically found in an equipment loan-type financing, other than possibly a lease that is in effect a conditional sale arrangement (where there is a one-dollar purchase option), it is possible to structure the arrangement to provide for an interim interest charge.

Prepayment Penalties

A typical net finance lease may not be canceled for any reason, thus guaranteeing the lease profits, subject, of course, to a lease default. Some prospective lessees, however, want the right to terminate a lease early if the equipment become obsolete or surplus to their needs or simply for convenience. The same may be true for equipment subject to a loan arrangement. This type of option, if granted, can be an opportunity for profit.

Generally, when a right to terminate a lease, or loan, early is granted, it is permitted only upon payment of an amount equal to a predetermined termination value, typically stated in a termination schedule. The termination payment is usually expressed as a percentage of equipment cost for each rent or loan payment period when a termination can be exercised. For example, a monthly lease might provide for a termination payment of 85% of equipment cost when the sixth rent payment is made, 83% of the equipment cost when the seventh rent payment is made, and so on. Properly structured, the payment of a lease termination value will return the entire remaining equipment cost investment, with the lessor's anticipated profits at least to the date of termination, and include funds to pay off any equipment purchase loans, any tax benefit recapture for taxes claimed, but not fully vested, and add as additional profit an exercise penalty. A similar result, as applicable, can be obtained with a loan prepayment.

Casualty Occurrences

An equipment casualty occurrence, in effect, ends a lease. In the same manner as a lessee-elected early lease termination, provision must be made for the protection of a lessor's investment, and profit, at least to the date of the casualty occurrence. The same can be true in the case of a conditional sale arrangement.

Typically, leases contain casualty loss provisions that require that the lessee pay a predetermined casualty value payment. These payments are usually prescribed by formula in a lease provision or in a casualty payment schedule, often expressed as a percentage of equipment cost, all specified to be backed up by property damage insurance, which must be taken out by the lessee. Casualty value payments, like termination payments, are designed to make a lessor economically whole, including payment for any remaining unpaid invested funds as well as the loss of anticipated tax benefits and, possibly, residual profits. For example, a monthly lease might provide, in the event of an equipment casualty occurrence during a specified rent payment period, for the payment of a casualty value amount equal to 98% of equipment cost anytime during the second rent payment period, 96% of equipment cost anytime during the third rent payment period, and so on.

In structuring an equipment casualty payment obligation, the lessor can build in a reasonable profit to compensate for loss of its long-term investment opportunity. When casualty payments are expressed as a percentage of equipment cost in a casualty payment schedule, one way to do this is to increase rock-bottom casualty loss payments by a small percentage, say 2% of the equipment cost, added to each specified casualty value percentage.

Insurance Cost Markups

Equipment insurance is a must in any equipment lease or loan, and, generally, the lessee, or borrower, is required to provide the specified coverage through its insurance carrier. Although care must be taken by a lessor not to run afoul of any insurance regulations, providing the insurance itself, and passing the cost on to the lessee, with a markup, can create another lease profit opportunity. For example, a lessor might charge 14 U.S. dollars a year for a 2,000 U.S. dollar casualty insurance policy costing 8 U.S. dollars a year, making a 6 U.S. dollars profit. On a 20,000,000 U.S. dollar equipment portfolio, this means 60,000 U.S. dollars annually.

A lessor with insurance volume purchasing power can offer equipment lease insurance at a markup while still providing rates equal to or lower than that available to most lessees or borrowers.

Another added benefit for a lessor or financing entity providing the insurance coverage is that it eliminates the need to administratively track compliance by the lessee or borrower of the insurance coverage requirement, an important aspect of any financing.

Upgrade Financing

Equipment upgrades, when a lessee or borrower adds to or modifies existing leased or financed equipment, can provide an opportunity for additional profit. If the upgrade is not readily removable or has no standalone value, generally, the existing lessor, or lender, is the only one willing or able to finance it. In these situations, the lessee, or borrower, has two choices: to purchase the upgrade with its own funds, in which case, in a lease situation, the upgrade may belong to the lessor at the end of the lease, or agree to whatever lease or financing rate the lessor or lender offers. If, as is the case in many lease situations, the upgrade is deemed, under the terms of the lease, to become the property of the lessor because, for example, it becomes an integral part of the leased equipment and cannot be removed without damage to the existing equipment, paying a higher financing cost may still be more advisable than purchasing an upgrade, which automatically becomes the lessor's property.

Documentation and Filing Fees

Many finance customers, particularly those leasing or financing small ticket items of equipment, such as small computer systems, will pay, with little or no objection, stated transaction processing, documentation preparation, and security interest filing fees. Small financing transaction documentation fees generally run from 50 to 500 U.S. dollars per transaction. Security interest filing fees, such as state Uniform Commercial Code filing fees, are generally nominal, ranging from 15 to 25 U.S. dollars. The more fees a lessee or borrower pays, the less a lessor's or lender's profit erosion.

Equipment Maintenance and Repair Charges

Requiring a lessee to pay for all normal equipment upkeep, such as maintenance and repair costs, protects a lessor's investment by ensuring that the lessor's profit and collateral value is not eroded by unexpected maintenance and repair costs if the equipment is returned. Simply, shifting the full cost burden of equipment maintenance and repair to a lessee eliminates or substantially lessens re-sale or re-lease refurbishment expenses if the equipment is returned at lease term end.

Product vendor lessors willing, and able, to provide equipment maintenance and repair service, even in connection with a finance lease, can derive another opportunity for additional profit through service charges. Many computer vendors, for example, offer these types of services and have created substantial collateral lease revenues.

Excess Use Charges

The better the condition leased equipment is in when returned, the greater the potential for the highest possible end-of-lease sale or re-lease profits. Another way to ensure the best possible return condition and ensure profits is to put use restrictions on the equipment, which, if exceeded, provide for penalty charges payable at the end of the lease, referred to as excess use charges. Automobile lessors typically have annual mileage limitations, which, if exceeded, require the lessee to pay additional rental charges to make up for potentially reduced end-of-lease sale or re-lease value. Leased aircrafts are also often subject to use restrictions in the form, for example, of remaining engine hours before the next required maintenance cycle or prescribing a maximum number of takeoff and landing cycles, which, if exceeded, impose added charges.

Re-Marketing Fees

Equipment re-marketing fees are another way for equipment lessors to increase lease profits. For example, a lease may require that the lessee pay a predetermined fee to the lessor if the lessee elects to terminate a lease early, or decides not to renew the lease and return the equipment at the end of the lease, to cover the lessor's cost to re-market (sell or re-lease) the equipment. These fees are in addition to any other charges that may be payable, such as termination penalties, or costs to repair the equipment to the condition required under the lease agreement.

Late Payment Charges

Leases and other financing contracts always incorporate late payment charges. If, for example, rent is not paid when due, there will be a penalty added to the late payment. Lessees often tolerate penalties in excess of the actual delayed payment time value of money cost. In fact, some late payment penalties are as high as 5 to 10% of the rent charge.

Collection Charges

Although not strictly a profit opportunity, requiring lessees or borrowers to pay for any cost of ensuring timely lease or loan payments, many lessors or lenders, particularly small ticket lessors or lenders, require that lessees or borrowers pay telephone charges on collection calls, as well as other collection charges, which could include the cost of a collection agency. Leases or loan arrangements can also include charges incurred for attorney collection fees. Anything that reduces overheard is indirectly a lessor or lender profit item.

Re-Delivery Charges

Equipment re-delivery charges are another area of lease profit opportunity. It is not unusual for a lessee to agree to return the leased equipment at the end of the lease to a designated return point, free of charge to the lessor. This enables a lessor selling or re-leasing the equipment to add a small profit amount by also charging the new user a delivery fee from the lessee's location of use. And, at times, some lessors get lessees to agree to pay for all such shipment charges, regardless of where in the world the equipment is shipped.

Summary

There are many components in product financing arrangements that can add profits, ranging from financing rates to end-of-lease term sales and re-leasing. Serious consideration should be given to building in the various profit components to ensure that a financing operation runs profitably.

CHAPTER 3

Evaluating the Establishment of a Product Vendor Third-Party Financing Program

Fully In-House or Third-Party Financing Program Options

There are two basic ways for a product vendor to establish a customer product financing program.

The first is to establish their own in-house financing operation, discussed in detail in Chapter 4. Typically, in the recent past, the setting up of an in-house financing operation by a product vendor was not considered a viable option because it required establishing from the ground up a specialized and fully functional operation, which included hiring a credit manager, an operations manager, legal counsel, a state and local sales and property tax manager, and document review specialists, in addition to acquiring extensive and costly software systems to process, monitor, manage, and report transactions, and the setting up of a contract billing and collection operation, all of which required a substantial personnel and cost commitment. Making the consideration for setting up an in-house financing activity even more challenging was the fact that all of this was not readily apparent to individuals not actually working in the equipment finance area. Today, as previously mentioned, fortunately for a product vendor interested in setting up an in-house financing profit center, many cost-effective options for an in-house setup exist that were not available even five years ago. Other considerations, however, discussed in this chapter may still cause a product vendor to take a different approach.

The second way for a product vendor to establish a customer product financing program is to enter into what is referred to as a *vendor program* arrangement with one or more third-party financing companies. This is a viable option if a product vendor determines, after considering all aspects, that they do not have financial resources or management available to run a fully in-house financing operation or simply would prefer not to operate a financing company, at least not initially. And, if there is any concern, rational or not, about setting up an in-house operation, this is a good first step because it will bring a product vendor up the financing learning curve in a manageable way. The downside in using an independent third-party leasing company in a vendor program arrangement is that it will eliminate financing profits, possible end-of-lease term re-leasing or sales profits and transaction flexibility that would otherwise be available from operating an in-house financing activity. A possible third hybrid alternative to either of the aforementioned approaches would be to explore setting up a financing joint venture with a third-party investor.

The Considerations

As a general rule, if you as a product vendor establish a fully functional in-house financing capability, a captive leasing and financing company, you are in the best position for obvious reasons: you control the financing product offerings, the financing decisions, the lease or financing documentation, and your products' off-lease sale or re-lease secondary market. Also, in addition to adding a new profit center, an in-house product leasing and financing capability is the right choice if you want to have any assurance that you will have the most effective type of customer financing program possible—one tailored to fit your particular type of customer's needs. However, as a general rule, for product vendors without financial and operational expertise or investment funds, the availability of experienced leasing company management (full time or on a consulting basis), and competitive debt arrangements, the better choice may be to establish a third-party *private label* vendor program, one where the third-party financing company offers customer financing under the product vendor's name, or a derivation thereof, as possibly the first step. This choice has its downside, as discussed later in this chapter; but, once you are comfortable with the process, then you can consider setting up a fully in-house financing operation.

If you as a product vendor decide to use a third-party financing company and set up a vendor program to service your customer financing needs, the financing company you use must be reliable and offer readily available financing for every type of prospective customer you may have. And, it is particularly important when working with a third-party financing company to independently verify this because their sales personnel often promise more than their operational personnel are able or willing to deliver. Not using a vendor program arrangement at a minimum with a third-party financing company and merely providing a prospective equipment customer with the name of an equipment financing company to talk to, or letting a prospective customer find its own financing, are not recommended approaches.

Key Elements in a Third-Party Financing Company Vendor Program Arrangement

If the decision is to rely on a third-party leasing or financing company vendor program to satisfy your product sales financing needs, possibly as the first step in developing an effective customer product financing program, the following are some important suggestions.

Establish Multiple Funding Relationships

In setting up a third-party financing company vendor program, it is important to establish vendor program relationships with more than one financing company because relying on one financing company to service all of your customers' financing needs is not recommended for many reasons. There have been many situations in which both bank-affiliated and non-bank leasing companies have closed their funding doors without warning and with indifference to vendor customer commitments, have become inflexible in meeting customer needs, decide that they no longer want to continue financing a vendor's products, or refuse to finance a certain type of customer, such as municipal or non-profit customers. In addition, one financing company's credit standards may not be broad enough to fit your prospective customer profile, something you may not discover until you run into a problem that you did not anticipate, or the financing company changes business direction, something that could negatively impact your customer financing program virtually overnight. So, establishing multiple funding relationships is essential and, generally, working with at least three financing companies is recommended if there could be any significant financing business volume.

The Program Should Be a Private Label

Other considerations aside, it is usually the best approach in establishing a third-party vendor program arrangement to have the financing company hold itself out as a part of your company through a seamless interface with your customers, including answering phone calls, responding to e-mails, and otherwise dealing with your customers as if the customers were dealing directly with your company, referred to as a *private label* program, using your company's name or a name denoting a financing activity provided by your company.

Understand and Control the Financing Process

It is always advisable for you, as a product vendor, to have a thorough understanding of how any third-party financing company you decide to work with makes its customer credit decisions, as well as to have substantial input into and management control over customer transaction interaction and documentation, including transaction processing, to ensure every transaction that can get done gets done. And, that means the following:

Develop an Agreed-Upon Set of Uniform Lease and Financing Documents

Developing one set of lease and financing documents, generally acceptable to all financing companies you are working with, is an important marketing step. If a deal is turned down by one financing company, because, for example, of document changes requested by your customer, new documents do not have to be re-signed to use for another financing source, saving time and possible loss of credibility, any of which can, and likely will, damage your customer relationship. Additionally, it is always advisable to agree beforehand what document changes may be acceptable to each financing company you are working so that you can handle any preliminary document negotiations. Finally, the documents should be in your company's name or a company name that denotes a financing activity provided by your company.

Get a Commitment on Credit Parameters and Financing Rates, in Writing

Make sure you have a clear agreement on what financing rates are available and what the indexing parameters are for rate changes will be going forward (such as what changes in the financing rates will occur for changes in prime rate). And, you should have clear agreement on what the basic credit hurdles will be for accepting a customer for financing, such as the number of necessary years in business and how many years of financial statements will be required. Nothing is more damaging to product marketing than going back to a new prospective or existing customer, after offering equipment financing at a given rate, and telling the customer, without any forewarning as to the possibility, that the financing rates have increased, or that they do not meet the financing credit requirements, particularly when the rate change or necessary credit parameters could have been anticipated or the reason for any turndown was something that another financing company would not have found objectionable.

Even if you have what appears to be a clear understanding to finance customers that meet certain financial and business standards from a third-party financing company, you should document the commitment in writing in a vendor program agreement. Otherwise, you may have no assurance of funding reliability. These commitments are typically filled with qualifications, ones that you should thoroughly understand because the commitments are rarely legally enforceable due to the qualifications and invariably subject to change with changing market conditions, all of which you should know in advance.

Manage the Key Aspects of the Document Process

Taking control of the lease or financing credit application and documentation process is important. This ensures problems will be properly addressed in a timely manner. For example, your salesperson should prepare, or monitor the preparation of, a pre-approved financing application and the pre-approved financing documents, submit them, when necessary, to your customer for ultimate submission to your financing company and then actively monitor the transaction weekly, or, if necessary, daily.

When Working with Third-Party Financing Companies, Conduct Preliminary Document Reviews

When using third-party financing companies to provide customer financing, to head off avoidable problems, you should conduct your own preliminary document *acceptability review* before submitting a transaction to the prospective financing company, making sure the documents were properly completed, and that no changes were made of which you were not aware. Very often, issues that could result in a turndown can be readily addressed to facilitate an approval before the application or financing documents are submitted to a financing company you are working with. Once a prospective customer is turned down by one financing company, it is more difficult to get a funding approval from another financing company. Even if the original turndown reason did not have a good basis, it is a fact of business that credit managers, at times, turn down a proposed transaction they may otherwise have accepted merely because the transaction was previously turned down by another financing company because of a concern that the previous credit manager identified a problem they could not find.

Avoid Providing Financial Guarantees

Be careful about generally providing financing guarantees for customer leases or other financing contracts requested by third-party finance companies. For example, a leasing company may suggest that if your company guarantees your customer's financing contracts all your customer financing transactions will always get done, at least up to a certain aggregate dollar amount. Financial guarantees can adversely affect your general growth and borrowing capabilities. Worse yet, many lease or other financing contract guarantees permit collection from the guarantor without having first exhausted all remedies against the contract obligor.

Investigate Prospective Third-Party Financing Company Backgrounds Thoroughly

The financial and business backgrounds of every third-party leasing and financing company you consider doing business with must be investigated thoroughly, and that includes determining their years in business, their ownership background, their financial capabilities, and their deal track record. Not doing so can create avoidable risks. For example, it is possible a selected leasing company simply will not have the money available to properly service your customer financing needs or is, in fact, a financing broker with no available funds of its own. An early investigation can prevent unfortunate surprises.

Be Skeptical About Dealing with Lease Investment Funds

Lease investment funds promoted by investment bankers and lease brokers surface from time to time. They are public or private investment partnerships that raise money to invest in equipment leases or financing arrangements. Historically, many have had problems as a result of poor management or improper structuring. And, when problems arise, funding is cut off. So, if you decide to work with an investment fund, do not rely on it exclusively for customer funding.

Summary

Setting up an in-house product financing activity has solid benefits, but only if a company has a market value-added reason for being in the financing business. If your company has such a reason, take time to carefully evaluate all aspects of leasing and financing as it may affect your potential operations. And, if you, as a product vendor, are unsure of committing to a full in-house financing operation, consider starting with a third-party financing program arrangement.

CHAPTER 4

Key Considerations for Setting Up an In-House Product Financing Operation

Establishing an In-House Financing Operation

For a product vendor, starting an in-house product financing company can be an involved process, but today, it is manageable using available resources. If you, as a product vendor, are considering establishing, or have decided to establish, a fully functional in-house equipment leasing and financing program, the material in this chapter will frame the various components you will need to address, discussed in greater detail in later chapters, as well as assist you in reaching a decision and in setting up any financing operation.

In making an initial assessment of the setting up a fully functional in-house customer financing operation, you will need to consider all the aspects of leasing and financing discussed in this book, such as the financial, document, tax, legal, accounting, structuring, and business issues. For example, you must consider the actual mechanics of starting and running a successful product financing operation. And, that must include the day-to-day administrative aspects, the source of the money needed for both your operation and the financing transactions, how to best market your customer financing, how to perform credit evaluations, how to develop and process documentation, how to monitor state sales and use tax compliance and payments, and how to handle any necessary financing payment delinquencies and equipment repossessions. Additionally, you should consider establishing a relationship with experienced outside legal counsel, if none is available internally, for preparing a user-friendly and enforceable set of form financing documents, as well as to work with in the event there are document negotiation issues or contract defaults, resulting in necessary customer collection actions or lawsuits. Finally, you should also consider hiring an experienced financing consultant to assist you in avoiding the many pitfalls that you may encounter if you do not have internal financing expertise available. While all of this at first may seem overwhelming, breaking it down into segments can make the setup operation extremely manageable.

The material following is an overview of the primary operational considerations necessary for the startup and day-to-day functioning of a customer financing operation. Because of the many possible individual company variables, however, you must also consider aspects that your company or product market may need to accommodate, something you will be better able to do after reading the material in this book.

Decide if You Should Use a Separate Business Financing Entity

Typically, product vendors who establish an in-house or a quasi-in-house (such as under a third-party vendor program) financing operation set it up in a separate entity or, at a minimum, under a name that denotes a separate financing activity, which would likely be considered a division, discussed in greater detail in Chapter 5. A division has no separate legal standing under the law and is, in fact, the same as the entity setting up the division. For example, Great Technology Corporation may establish its activity under a DBA (doing business as) name, such as Great Technology Leasing, which in effect would be thought of as company division. Simply, financing contracts entered under the name Great Technology Leasing as a DBA name would be legally considered to have been entered into by Great Technology Corporation. That means that all contract-related obligations, and any equipment ownership, reside in the main entity; in this case, Great Technology Corporation. So, for example, if your financing contracts, or their receivables, are sold to a third-party financing company, Great Technology Corporation, and not a separate legal entity that could have been set up to run the financing operation, would incur any liability arising in connection with the financing contracts, or their receivables, sales. That may not be objectionable, but something to consider. If, on the other hand, a separate financing legal entity, such as a corporate entity, was set up as, say, a wholly owned subsidiary, all financing-related obligations and liabilities would, other considerations aside such as required parent company guarantees, be limited to the financing entity. In any event, from a tax and accounting viewpoint, any approach would likely have, on a consolidated basis, the same accounting and tax implications.

Basic State Law Considerations

If you decide to set up a separate financing entity, you must determine what state to organize your financing entity in and then consider what states in which you must qualify that organization to do financing business in; otherwise, at a minimum, the courts in the states you do not so qualify will not be available to you in the event you need to sue a defaulting financing customer. Additionally, the various applicable laws of the states in which you intend to do business must be checked to determine what statutory language, if any, must be included in lease and financing agreements, as well as what, if any, state licensing requirements may be necessary for any financing activity and what interest rate limitations may exist. An experienced finance lawyer will be instrumental in bringing the legal considerations into focus for your business operation.

What are Your Current Internal Business Capabilities?

If you believe that setting up a fully functional, in-house product financing operation is the direction you want to go in, an important consideration will be to determine your basic marketing and profit objectives for setting it up and then, assessing any existing equipment leasing and financing management, operational and financial capabilities you may have internally. Depending on the answers, you may initially decide to enter into a vendor program relationship with one or more independent leasing companies, as suggested in Chapter 3, or, for more control and to establish a new profit center, you may determine that it would be best to pursue actually establishing a fully functional, in-house captive leasing and financing operation. If you decide to set up a fully functional in-house operation, you will want to conceptually design a customer financing program that will be responsive to your prospective customer financing requirements. And then, determine how to handle the various transaction process requirements discussed as follows, a critical element in maximizing the benefits of offering customer equipment financing. Additionally, as already stated, you should consider and evaluate using various cost-effective third-party resources for operational aspects that you do not have, or do not want to take on, internally, outlined as follows.

Identify any Necessary Financial Support

Determining what your source will be for the money required for your customer financing is a key consideration if you plan to set up an in-house financing operation. If it is determined that, in effect, you will wait for your financing revenues to come in for your product sales and financing profits, in effect using internal funds, then, as long as you have the funds necessary to wait and you are not concerned with income recognition for financial reporting purposes at the time of the product financing, your decision is simple. If not, then you will need to determine how to obtain the money necessary for your financing transactions, something that can be done by arranging, or using, a business line of credit, putting in place an arrangement where you will immediately discount (borrow against) all financing contract receivables with a third-party financing company or putting in place an arrangement where you immediately sell the equipment and the financing contracts to a third-party financing company, all discussed in in greater detail in Chapter 5. Something to keep in mind, however, is that the discounting of your contract receivables, if they are not subject to net finance leases or loan contracts, may require some form of financial support, which in turn may impact your ability to recognize income received immediately, an issue for your accountants. For example, if your financing contact is a managed services or fee-per-use agreement, as discussed in Chapter 9, you may need to either provide an indemnity or buyback commitment for possible payment termination by the customer prior to the end of the financing term based on a claim, for example, of service non-performance and put up a letter of credit if your business credit is not sufficient to cover any possibly termination liability. Finally, and of course something generally not viewed as the best route would be to bring in a third-party investor to provide operating funds for the in-house operation and financing activity.

Administrative Issues

If you intend to set up an in-house financing activity, you must establish the necessary administrative processes to carry out all aspects of the financing operation. And, that includes credit review and processing, document review and processing, security interest filings (discussed in Chapter10), tracking and payment of applicable state product sales and use taxes, rent invoicing, ongoing new business marketing of existing customers, new prospect marketing, invoice collection, accounting, equipment repossession and re-sale or re-leasing, and lawsuit initiation and monitoring. Toward this end, there now exist a wide variety of computer software programs available that can facilitate many of the tracking and processing activities, such as, for example, lessor rent pricing, and documentation, as mentioned in Chapter 1. Additionally, as discussed in Chapter 6, there are now many third-party service providers who offer billing, collection, and report generation services, such as Orion First (www.orionfirst.com). That is, basically, all key functions, other than credit determinations that fall outside of pre-approved parameters, can be done using acquired software and outsourced services, making the establishment of an in-house financing activity both cost-effective and manageable in today's business environment.

Establish Overall Customer Relationship Objectives

The overall objectives for an effective equipment financing program are obvious; yet, time and time again, they not are given enough attention in the rush to set up the operation and put business on the books. For example, everyone agrees that maintaining good customer relations and offering an effective product financing process are essential business objectives; yet, many equipment vendors jeopardize their objectives once a third-party leasing company is involved, either because the financing company is providing financing under a vendor program arrangement or are otherwise providing funds for financed contracts, by not maintaining some aspect of control over the process. One large U.S. leasing company was well known for aggressively and effectively establishing vendor program relationships with equipment vendors. And, their customer service and administration departments were equally well known to people in the industry for aggressively, and inadvertently, damaging customer relationships through inflexibility, inattention, and indifference to product vendor customer relationships.

Determine What Products You Want to Offer for Financing

The ideal type of product to provide lease financing for is capital equipment that has a long useful life, a life that is typically much longer than the contemplated lease terms, typically three to seven years. Computer equipment often becomes technologically obsolete in a relatively short period and generally does not fit into this category. On the other hand, rail cars, aircraft, and hydrogen fuel cells are examples of assets that fit this category. However, assets not having relatively long useful lives or end-of-financing term re-marketing potential, such as computer equipment, can also provide a solid financing opportunity, particularly if the financing involves equipment that is essential to a customer's operation (referred to as *essential-use equipment*), or the transaction is structured properly to offset any potential end-of-lease sale or re-leasing downside. For example, generally, leased equipment that is essential-use equipment even with a short useful life is more likely to be renewed or purchased by the customer at lease term end than equipment not within that category. Also, equipment with a short useful life can have, if the lease term is 60 to 70% of its estimated useful life, good end-of-lease residual value giving you as a lessor the opportunity for added profits by selling or re-leasing the equipment at lease term end for a reasonable dollar amount.

Determine What Your Financing Rates will be

In setting up an in-house product financing operation, you will need to estimate what financing rates you will use, after assessing your cost of money and your estimated operating costs, all considering your marketing objectives. And, in setting the financing rates, you should determine if there is enough profit margin in your product sales price to absorb a narrow financing profit, ideally considering any proceeds you anticipate receiving from end-of-lease equipment sales or re-leases. End-of-lease equipment sales and re-leasing, as discussed in Chapter 2, can be a major component in the profitability of any financing activity. Once both your cost of money, transaction operating costs, and financing rates are estimated, you should, as a starting point, develop a business income projection as a general guide, adjusting periodically in real time by actual income and costs as you proceed. Realistically, it is not possible to develop a pro forma profit and loss projection that is 100% accurate, so this exercise is simply a good starting point to ensure all aspects of an operation are considered.

Estimating Your Deal Cost: What to Consider

It should go without saying that before you can estimate your customer financing pricing, you will need to determine your cost of money for any financing offered and the administrative cost of each individual financing transaction. Identifying your raw cost of money may be nothing more than determining the interest rate on funds borrowed from your bank under, say, your general line of credit. The transaction administrative cost of your financing operation that should be allocated to each transaction would include the cost of any credit processing software, transaction processing software, and back-office administrative servicing costs. These contract costs may also be equally easy to identify, particularly if you are outsourcing billing and collecting financing invoices to a third-party service provider and you are using third-party software to evaluate and process prospective transactions.

A Financing Rate Rule of Thumb

Although there are no simple ways to determine what financing rate may be acceptably charged your prospective financed customers, there is a rule of thumb you can start with, one that is used by a few high-volume leasing companies that anticipate solid end-of-lease residual profits in setting their financing rates. And, that is done by generally marking up their cost of money by 350 to 400 basis points (3.5 to 4%), an estimate they have developed internally to be used to comfortably cover their operating cost and generate a profit. Using this type of *rule of thumb* approach would need periodic verification at each fiscal year end, if not quarterly, to ensure your financing activity is, in fact, running at a profit. The higher the financing volume of business you do, the more likely you will cover operating cost and become solidly profitable.

Consider Market Competition

Another important consideration in setting up an in-house financing program is determining what your competitors are doing. That is, do they also offer product financing directly or through third-party financing companies, and, if so, what document structures, rates, and terms are they offering? One aspect of a product financing activity to always keep in mind is that the financing rates you offer your product customers can be the determining factor on which your customer decision maker makes his or her decision, particularly when your product competitor is also offering a similar product. So, in establishing your financing activity, gathering some market intelligence on what competitive financing rates are in your industry for various sized deals is very important. If that information is not readily available, it can often be obtained during your customer sales calls. Customers are often willing to disclose competitive rates, even if nothing more than to negotiate what financing rate you are willing to offer. Another excellent way to determine market rate information is to talk to potential financing companies that may be willing to take your customer referrals, or otherwise participate in your transactions. In any event, you do not want to underprice your product financing, unless that is part of your product sales build strategy, understanding that financing rates for various product types and industries vary, at times, widely.

Pricing Your Finance Deals with Product Sales Profits

Notwithstanding what financing rates you charge, as a product vendor, you have an important component to work with in marketing your products and setting your financing rates that is not available to stand-alone third-party financing companies: the profit margin on your products. So, conceptually, if you want to increase sales, it is not unrealistic for you to initially consider offering your financing at breakeven rates to start, relying more on your product profit markup, anticipating an increase in profits from additional product sales and from end-of-lease term product sales or re-leases in the secondary market.

Build in Solid Sales Incentives

There is no doubt that compensation drives sales, and as a component of financing activity overhead, you should seriously consider instituting a solid sales commission incentive for the financing activity, something, at times, executives have difficulty with if the financing sales activity could generate substantial commissions for the sales personnel resulting in a feeling they are being *paid too much*. That, however, is a short-sight business viewpoint.

Prospective Customer Credit Evaluations are Critical

As part of setting up your transaction processing procedure, a credit processing channel will need to be established, incorporating your minimum acceptance credit criteria, ideally intergraded with your transaction processing software so that credit decisions can generally be automatically made for transaction up, say, to 250,000 U.S. dollars. Establishing your credit assessment criteria will likely require the services of an experienced credit manager, full time or on a part time or consulting basis, to determine your basic credit parameters and to provide you with information on how to assess any data that may vary from your ideal credit targets parameters set in your credit processing software, all as discussed in Chapter 6.

What Happens if a Financed Customer Goes Bankrupt?

You should develop a plan and the necessary legal contacts in the event a customer becomes subject to reorganization or liquidation under the bankruptcy laws, discussed in Chapter 15.

Tax and Accounting Implications

Every lease and financing transaction has tax implications for a product vendor's in-house financing activity. These implications can vary depending on the changes in the terms and conditions of a lease or other financing transaction. For example, offering a one U.S. dollar purchase option at the end of a lease term changes the lease from a true lease for income tax purposes, where the lessor is entitled to claim equipment depreciation, and, if available, any investment tax credits, to a conditional sale, where the *lessor* is deemed to be an equipment lender, and, thereby, not entitled to the equipment ownership tax benefits, as discussed in Chapter 11.

The characterization of lease or other financing transaction for accounting purposes, discussed in Chapter 8, can also affect your financial statements, and your accountants must be brought early into the consideration discussions to assist in understanding the financial reporting effect various lease and financing structures will have on existing business financial statements given to shareholders, investors, or your banks.

An Effective Deal Processing Procedure is Essential

As will be discussed in Chapter 6, in setting up an in-house financing program, you will need to establish a well-defined transaction processing procedure, ideally using state-of-the-art financing software readily available in the marketplace to process credit, proposals, and financing contracts. A good example of this type of software is offered by Terra Vista Software (https://terravistasoftware.com), based in Orinda, California.

Assessing and Developing What Product Financing Documents to Use

The type of documentation you will need will depend on the type of transactions to be offered, such as, for example, a lease, a conditional sale agreement, a managed services agreement, or a fee-per-use agreement, all discussed in Chapter 9.

The most basic and common form of equipment financing agreement is a lease agreement. Today, it is often written in customer-friendly plain

English, minimizing legal jargon that would make it difficult to understand by business personnel. The next most common form of financing document is a conditional sale agreement, which is essentially a product purchase loan arrangement. These are also now often written in plain English for the same reason as with customer-friendly lease agreements.

In general, you may only need a short-form lease contract (single transaction and master lease formats) and a short-form conditional sale contract (single transaction and master formats), to start, unless, of course, you want to also offer services and collateral products, in which case, you will need to develop forms that cover so-call bundled equipment and services or collateral packages. A sample short-form single transaction lease has been included in the Appendix.

Very simply, the short-form documents you develop should enable you to handle transactions up to 250,000 to 1,000,000 U.S. dollars, and possibly higher, depending on the comprehensive nature of the provisions. The nature and length of each document will depend on the dollar amount of financing involved and the type of product financing that will be offered, so experienced financing legal counsel should be retained as part of the development of the form documents.

Once the short-form documents that will be needed have been developed, they, if possible, should be uploaded into any financing processing software so that the applicable customer information will be automatically populated into the required documents if a customer decides to accept an offered product financing.

In addition to a short-form, single transaction lease, and a short-form master lease agreement with accompanying schedule, you should also, if the dollar amount of your product sales is or could be high, develop a form lease and master agreement and schedule for *large ticket* financings, typically far in excess of one million U.S. dollars, and, if you sell software, possibly a software license financing agreement, typically called an installment payment agreement. To the extent that any services, or disposables, are to be provided, along with capital equipment, managed services and fee-per-use forms of agreements should also be developed. Often, managed services or fee-per-use agreements are very attractive to product users for a variety of reasons, including the possibility of favorable accounting treatment, discussed in Chapter 8.

Typically, traditional financing documents are written, so they are non-cancelable for the financing term and, as such, make it easy to get favorable outside financing for by, for example, selling the contract receivables to a third-party financing company. Managed services and fee-per-use agreements can be subject to customer termination because, for example, of the real or claimed non-performance of related services or product supply obligations, something that may be upheld in a court of law. Accordingly, as suggested earlier, these types of contracts can be difficult and sometimes impossible to obtain financing for from bank-affiliated leasing companies or independent financing companies that do not know how to structure the financing arrangement to eliminate the clear legal deficiencies often present in these documents or that have not come to terms with accepting the associated business risks of financing non-traditional contract forms. This contract *flaw*, again, however, can typically be remedied by the product vendor guaranty the disposable or supply commitment and any servicing performance, as suggested earlier in this chapter.

Once you assess what you are trying to competitively achieve, there are times when a financing document can be designed specifically to fit the product being sold, that is, to consider a hybrid financing document. These documents, for various reasons, need to be developed with legal and financing personnel that understand the needs of the banking or other financing community if you want to leverage your product financing investment with third-party debt or selling the contracts to a third-party financing company.

In addition to the base documents discussed earlier, you should also develop form collateral documents, such as a form of guarantee and corporate or organizational certificates, that might be needed or advisable, all of which are discussed in Chapter 10.

Finally, the legal strength and provision term flexibility of the financing documents are critical to the success of a financing activity, particularly important in the case of legal strength when it is necessary to sue and collect from a defaulting financing customer or, as discussed earlier, to raise financing investment capital. If, for example, you intend to assign a customer lease as security for financing a transaction loan, your agreements must contain effective assignment clauses, as well as other important provisions, including what is referred to as a hell or high-water provision. The reader is referred to Chapter 9 for a discussion of lessor assignment, and hell or high-water provisions.

Your Documents Must Comply with Applicable Law to be Enforceable

You must make sure that your financing contracts are drafted in a manner that they will be legally enforceable, discussed in Chapter 9. And, that means, among other aspects, verifying that the documents comply with any applicable laws, including any usury laws, in the jurisdictions where they will be used.

Your Documents will Require an Investment

Developing a good financing agreement together will require an upfront investment for legal advice, but it is well worth it. Investing thousands or even millions of dollars using, for example, a lease copied from a third-party lessor or competitor is not advisable.

Summary

Starting an in-house product financing company for someone unfamiliar with a financing operation can be challenging, but, today, using available third-party sources, it is a manageable process. A product vendor considering establishing a fully functional in-house equipment leasing and financing program should consider all the aspects of leasing and financing, such as the financial, document, tax, legal, accounting, structuring, and business issues.

CHAPTER 5

In-House Financing Program Structural Steps: The Basics

Setting Up Your Financing Entity

Once you, as a product vendor, decide to develop a product financing activity, you will need to decide where the financing activity will be based and whether it will be operated out of a separate affiliated company or your existing company, as mentioned in Chapter 4. Generally, any internal considerations aside, it should be set up in a separate affiliated legal entity. Doing so isolates your main business from any financing or financing-related liabilities that may arise, such as any transaction debt obligations or equipment-related liabilities from personal injury lawsuits. There are various organizational structures that can be used, discussed as follows.

Corporation

One of the most common financing organizational structures is the corporate entity. Any potential liability incurred by the corporate entity does not flow through to its shareholders. Other than using a division approach, discussed next, this is often the organization structure recommended and used for a financing affiliate operation.

Setting up a new corporate entity is easy and is accomplished by filing in the desired state the required organizational papers. So, if this is your choice, you need to decide what state to organize it in. If your product sales activities are throughout the United States and you want to offer financing for all your products, the best choice may be to set your financing entity up as a Delaware corporate entity, which you would then qualify to do business in the various jurisdictions where there may be financing activities. Qualification to do business in a state or other jurisdiction is simple and is typically done by filing the certificate of organization with the applicable jurisdictional agency. If the financing activities are to be limited to one state, then you can set up the corporate entity in that state, to limit the amount of organizational qualification that needs to be put into place.

Limited Liability Company

A limited liability company (LLC) may be used if you want to have corporate-like liability protection, but partnership treatment for income tax purposes, where all income and expenses flow through to the owner or owners of the LLC. Typically, a startup vendor financing entity that involves one or more third-party investors providing operational funds will consider using this structure, but it can also be used when no third parties are involved. At any later point in time, the LLC can be converted into a corporate entity. The organizational setup is accomplished by filing in the desired jurisdiction the required organizational papers and, as needed, filing the certificate of organization with the various applicable jurisdictional agencies where you intend to do business.

Limited Partnership

A limited partnership is another organization entity that can be considered in addition to an LLC when third-party investors are involved. The structure consists of one or more general partners and one or more investor limited partners. Each limited partner's liability is limited to their investment, and this arrangement, properly done, can be structured to allocate equipment ownership tax benefits in a predetermined and desirable manner. Each general partner, and often there is only one, which, in this case, would likely be the product vendor or an affiliate of the product vendor, however, is generally liable, something that can be limited by setting up any concerned non-product vendor-affiliate or product vendor-affiliate general partner as a corporate entity with a minimum net worth. The organizational setup is accomplished by filing in the desired jurisdiction the required organizational papers and, as needed, filing the certificate of organization with the various applicable state jurisdictional agencies where you intend to do business.

General Partnership

A general partnership structure for the financing activity, when there may be multiple participants, is generally not recommended for use even when there are third-party investors involved. Each party would have unlimited liability for anything that goes wrong as well as any obligations incurred. The setup is accomplished by simply developing a partnership agreement, acceptable to all parties and then, verify in those states you plan to do business what filing requirements may be required.

A Division

A division in the true sense of the term is not a recognized separate legal entity, and using a division as the financing entity is in effect the same as if the financing activity were run directly out of the product vendor entity and, thus, it exposes the product vendor using the division approach to direct liability for any negligence or damage lawsuit, as well as any other obligations incurred. There are generally no jurisdictional required organizational steps required for a division setup, assuming your main business entity is properly qualified, other than filing as necessary for any DBA (doing business as) name for your division.

Picking the Right Entity Name

It should go with saying that any financing activity should be operated under a financing name for marketing purposes. As a general rule, *finance*, *financial*, *bank*, or *banking* should not be used by a product vendor in any financing entity name. Some states, like New York, prohibit the use of these terms in the business name unless it is cleared with their Banking Department, an unnecessary complication. Generally, the use of *leasing*, *capital,* or similar words do not create a state regulatory or other compliance issue.

Setting Up Funding for Your Financing Operation

As discussed in Chapter 4, a key consideration in the setting up of a product vendor in-house financing operation is determining where the money will come from which is necessary for operating the financing activity, including the money necessary to fund the product financings. This, of course, assumes you, as a product vendor, do not want to fully self-fund your operation and rely, in part, on periodic financing payments coming in over the term of the financing contracts.

What might be your financing funding alternatives? It turns out that there are many to work with, other than fully funding your financing activity with internal funds, including setting up a bank line of credit for financing your transactions. You could, for example, set up a joint venture with an investor, allocating, for example, available equipment tax benefits to the investor, as well as a portion of the joint venture profits that result from the interest and residual components of each financing, or you could establish an arrangement with a third-party financing company to either purchase outright your financing contacts and any related applicable equipment or purchase (by discounting) your financing contract receivables. The advantages and disadvantages are, in most cases, apparent, but all of this should be discussed with your accountants and tax advisors.

If internal funds or a bank line of credit is used solely in a lease financing transaction, there are some accounting and tax considerations that must be taken into account, such as what ownership tax benefits are available and how and to what extent the income is to be financially reported in the case of product transfers to the financing operation. If you decide to raise funds by either selling outright your financing contacts and any related applicable equipment or selling (discounting) the contract receivables, there will be other implications that your accountants will need to address, including what amounts may be booked (reported) in your financial statements. Not properly addressing the accounting issues may significantly and adversely impact your reported earnings and financial ratios.

Using Internal Funds or a Bank Line of Credit

A detailed analysis of how to determine the impact for a product vendor in using internal funds or a bank line of credit to finance its product customers is beyond the scope of this book and, clearly, this is an assessment that has many variables that are dependent on a company's needs. But, either approach is a viable consideration for companies that are financially strong.

Financing Customer Deals with Third-Party Debt

Properly drafted financing contracts can be readily financed with third-party debt based upon the contract payment receivables over the financing term, and, if the customer's credit is acceptable, the debt can be on a nonrecourse basis to a product vendor. This approach allows a product vendor to in effect *sell* the contract receivables and report the *sale* income for accounting purposes. In other words, the contract receivables, but not the equipment ownership, are sold (borrowed against) on a discounted (present value) basis using the lender's lending interest rate, and if the receivables are sold on a nonrecourse basis, you, as a product vendor, will have no repayment responsibility if your customer defaults on their financing contract payments. The sale can be negotiated on a nondisclosed to the financed customer basis, subject to customer disclosure of the sale by the lender, or a product vendor optional repurchase, in the case of a customer contract default, with customer billing and collecting to be under your financing operation's name.

In the case of nonrecourse debt, as suggested earlier, if your financed customer defaults on the financing payments, you, as a product vendor, would not be responsible for the debt repayment, but, if the lender forecloses on your financed customer, the value of the equipment, which forms a portion of the loan collateral, will not be available to you other than, possibly, in a subordinated position to the lender. The advantages for a product vendor in selling contract receivables is that they will receive, at the time of debt financing, a lump sum payment equal to the present value of the financing payments discounted by the debt interest rate and still, if the financing is in the form of a lease, retain equipment ownership at the end of the financing term. So, for example, if your customer's lease rate is 7% per annum and the lease rate was computed using a zero end-of-lease-term equipment value (that is, the financing payments completely pays down the financed product purchase price) and the debt rate was 5% per annum, you would receive an interest profit (spread) in addition to, in effect, the financed product sales price (to the extent that the contract rents were priced with no end-of-contract residual value), and, if done properly, still own the equipment at the end of the lease, giving you the possibility of additional profits from the sale or re-lease of the equipment at the end of the lease term.

Financing Customer Deals by Selling Them to Third Party or Bank-Affiliated Financing Companies

Another viable alternative, but one with some profit limitations in the case of leases, is to sell a financing contract and related equipment to a third-party or bank-affiliated leasing company, something that is a possibility in today's market. The sale can be negotiated on a non-disclosed to the financed customer basis, subject to customer disclosure of the sale to the purchaser, or a product vendor optional repurchase, in the case of a customer contract default, with customer billing and collecting to be under the name of your financing operation. The downside to doing this, in the case of leases, is that you will lose any end-of-term equipment residual profit, something that may not be undesirable if you are looking for early cash income or the residual (end of lease term) value of the equipment is marginal. If the equipment residual value has some profit upside possibility, part of the sale negotiation may include your right to re-market the equipment at lease end and share in any end-of-lease equipment sale or re-leasing receivables.

Using a Third-Party Investor

Another approach, often not as desirable, is for a product vendor to bring into the financing operation a third-party investor by setting up a joint venture arrangement. This, of course would likely result, depending on the negotiated arrangement, in a loss to the product vendor of a portion of the equity and income value of the financing activity but may be a way to monetize the equipment ownership tax benefits available if they cannot be timely used by the product vendor. Once again, the accounting and tax issues must be assessed. This option would likely not be attractive option for large, profitable companies.

Establish an Equipment Re-Marketing Strategy

No matter how you, as a product vendor, set up the financing for your financing activity, using internal or, in whole or in part, third-party funds, to maximize profits, you must have a marketing strategy for available used products at the end of all lease contract terms. And, that may require the internal development of a marketing activity for used equipment, if you do not already have one, starting with existing customer contacts, and, if the equipment is sold to a third-party financing company along with the financing contracts, the negotiation of a re-marketing agreement that provides for a sharing of any end-of-lease (residual) equipment sale or re-leasing profits.

Summary

The first step, if you, as a product vendor, decide to set up a financing operation, whether an in-house operation or one using a third-party financing company vendor programs, is to establish an entity through which your financing operation will be run. And, that entity may be a corporation, an LLC, a limited partnership, a general partnership, or a division, all of which have pros and cons, depending on your specific needs. Additionally, you will want to develop a financing strategy for funding your customer financing transactions, as well as develop an end-of-lease term re-marketing strategy for off-lease equipment.

CHAPTER 6

Putting Your Credit and Administrative Process in Place

An Overview

If you, as a product vendor, have decided that an in-house financing operation will benefit your company, then you will need to develop a checklist of what operational items you will need to address, including what items you believe that you can handle with existing internal resources, what areas you will need to hire expert consultants for, and what items you initially believe you will want to outsource to third-party providers. Critical to your financing operation will be the development of your credit and your finance contract administration, all of which are discussed as follows. Some suggestions for hiring outside consultants are also provided.

Develop a Customer Sale Proposal that Includes a Financing Quote

In connection with developing a customer credit process, because an on-the-spot financing offer provided at the time of product sale is an effective way to move a purchase decision forward quickly, you will want to develop a financing proposal, one that, if accepted, will start the credit evaluation process. If the financing offer is not included in the product sale proposal, then you should develop a short, one-page financing offer letter to accompany the product sale proposal. The financing offer should contain a consent to review the customer's credit if it is a privately held company.

Your financing proposal should provide information for online access to a required credit application. The financing offer should have a short, two- to three-week period, for customer acceptance. And, consideration should be given to indexing any financing payment offered against a market index, such as a change in the prime rate, if the equipment delivery time would stretch beyond 60 to 90 days. For example, for every incremental percentage increase in the prime rate (or other applicable rate), the financing payment would increase by an equivalent percentage.

Setting Up Your Credit Process

An important, if not the most important, element in the setting up of an in-house vendor financing operation will be to ensure that your credit process is well thought through and implemented. This includes how you are going to mechanically set the credit process in motion, what credit agencies you will work with, and how you will process and review credit applications.

Credit Processing

Clearly, a key component of establishing an in-house financing activity is the setting up of a credit process that is effective, considers credit risks, and can process credit inquiries quickly. Decisions generally for deals under 1,000,000 U.S. dollars should be made in a matter of one or two days maximum after all necessary financial and other credit information is received or available, and possibly even hours, rather than weeks, if you want your financing process to be marketing-orientated. Here again, you should take advantage of existing third-party software, such as that offered by Terra Vista, referenced in Chapter 1, to process the credit application online, which software should also include the automatic issuance of an acceptance letter if the customer's is credit approved.

Do You Need an Experienced Credit Manager?

An important element to survival in the leasing and financing business is having the ability to properly assess the credit risks of entering into leases or other forms of financing contracts with prospective customers. Therefore, if your company does not have the internal ability to evaluate customer financing credit risks, you must acquire the expertise by hiring a credit manager or credit consultant. And, you should keep in mind that the credit approach for leasing to, or financing equipment for, a small business is dramatically different than leasing or financing equipment for Fortune 100 companies.

Something also to keep in mind when hiring a credit consultant or full-time expert is that someone able to effectively evaluate the creditworthiness of a Fortune 100 company may not be able to make an effective credit evaluation of a small business. No matter how much credit information you are able to obtain on any one customer, invariably, there are issues that will call for a credit risk judgment, sometimes a common sense judgment, and someone who has successfully reviewed hundreds, possibly more, credit files will bring a wealth of invaluable decision experience to an operation. Very simply, credit decisions are often an art rather than a science, calling for experienced judgment based on a solid track record. And, typically, that can come only from someone with a background of at least five or more years of credit decision experience.

A Basic Credit Primer

As aforementioned, a prospective financing customer's creditworthiness is one of the most important considerations in any decision to provide product financing. If the prospective customer's credit is weak, financial support from a parent company or other third-party may be the only way to provide the financing, and that clearly would be the only way for you to secure nonrecourse financing or sell the financing contract to a third-party financing company.

A comprehensive discussion of how to evaluate the credit standing of a prospective lessee or borrower is not possible because of the many variables that can be encountered, but it will be beneficial as a working frame of reference to go over some basic considerations, keeping in mind that what may create a credit problem for one financing company may not create a credit problem for another. For example, leasing companies with in-depth equipment knowledge and equipment re-marketing expertise may be more willing to overlook the typical credit concerns of a leasing company without this expertise. So, for you, as a product vendor with a financing activity, your equipment knowledge, coupled with any re-marketing expertise, can be an important factor as a part of your credit assessments.

In reviewing a prospective company's credit strength, there are many factors that are typically considered, including its assets and liabilities, cash flow, years in business, management strength, market presence, bank balances, and the dollar size of the requested financing. Large publicly held companies are the easiest to evaluate because there is ample and reliable evaluation information publicly available, such as audited financial statements that have been prepared by, generally, nationally recognized accounting firms, as well as from other publicly available material on file, say, with the Securities and Exchange Commission. And, in many cases, these companies have been *rated* for investment purposes by investment rating services, such as Moody's and Standard and Poor's rating services. In addition, valuable credit information can also be obtained from companies such as Dun and Bradstreet. Certainly, you will want access to this information as part of any credit assessment. Some suggestions for credit agencies are listed in the Appendix.

To give you a working frame of reference for the various aspects of the credit evaluation process, let us look at the criteria used in a simple credit evaluation—that for a small business. These types of *credits* are some of the hardest to evaluate. The following criteria are ones used by a small to lower mid-sized transaction leasing company whose equipment lease transactions range from 5,000 U.S. dollars to 250,000 U.S. dollars.

Minimum Time in Business. The applicant must have a minimum verifiable time in business of two years. Three years is required in the case of applications over 25,000 U.S. dollars, and four years in the case of applications over 100,000 U.S. dollars.

Existing Banking Relationship. The applicant must have a business bank relationship of at least two years, and the bank account must show a minimum low four-figure average balance. In the case of transactions exceeding 25,000 U.S. dollars, the minimum average account balance must be in the low five figures. There cannot be any overdrafts or check returns for insufficient funds.

Trade References. The applicant must provide three significant trade references, each of whose relationship goes back at least six months. COD trade references will not be acceptable.

Good Personal Credit. Personal credit reports must be forthcoming from the owners of the business that contain no derogatory information.

Financial Statements. Current assets must exceed current liabilities, and there must be a minimum equity to be determined by market conditions and deal size. [It should be noted that in today's market environment, typically leasing companies only require financial statements to be supplied for transactions exceeding 150,000 U.S. dollars, and, in the past few years, a number of leasing companies have raised that requirement to transactions exceeding 250,000 U.S. dollars.]

As you can see, there are a variety of factors to be considered.

What Type of Credit Agencies Should You Contract With?

There are many credit agencies that can supply information that will be needed in making credit evaluations, but it is advisable for you to contract with a few agencies to ensure that you have obtained the most comprehensive customer credit information available.

In many cases, the choice of what credit reporting agencies to contract with will be that of the credit manager, but some to consider, depending on the customer market intended to be pursued are: Experian (www.experian.com), PayNet (www.paynet.com), Dunn and Bradstreet (www.dnb.com), and Hoovers (www.hoovers.com). Generally, it is advisable to use more than one credit agency because doing so will allow you to cross-check the information and, in some cases, you will find that more detailed information is available from a particular credit agency that may fit your particular needs. Their services are offered on a monthly, sometime annual, basis and, in some cases, there is an additional per inquiry charge. Additionally, there are credit agencies that specialize in certain industry areas, such as the health-care area, that should be used if that is, in whole or in part, your customer base.

Credit Decisions Should Consider Current and Anticipated Economic Conditions

There is no doubt that making credit decisions must consider the current state of the economy and, as suggested earlier, the state of the industry in which your potential customer is operating. And, you should evaluate any economic trends, such as if the economy is heading downward or is projected to head downward. For example, some industry areas experience cyclic downturns, such as the rail industry, and, in these cases, you must evaluate and set strategies for managing credit risks in light of any trends, by, for example, ensuring there is sufficient collateral to offset any potential contract default or limiting your credit exposure to a comfortable dollar amount. Some credit agencies, such as PayNet, offer industry trend information that is extremely useful in making an evaluation.

Approaching Credit Decisions from a Common Sense Viewpoint

As stated earlier, particularly in the earlier stages of an in-house financing activity, when you are trying to augment your product sales marketing activity, you will want to take a common sense approach to evaluating a customer's credit. For example, if your customer is a municipality, such as a city, that has been in existence for 100 years and whose credit data does not meet your benchmark criteria, such as having a Paydex score five points below a minimum target of 65, the measure you have set for accepting financing for a customer, in making your decision, you should take into account the unlikelihood of the city defaulting on its payment obligations because of long-term cash flow problems and how critical the equipment is that you are providing for its operation. For example, financing equipment that might be considered essential-use equipment, such as for payroll processing, building lighting, or building power backup, is less likely to have a payment default.

Repeat Customer Payment Histories are Invaluable

As your in-house financing activity progresses and you have repeat financing customers, their payment history will be invaluable; keeping in mind that companies can experience industry market downturns, so anticipating what could happen in a particular industry is extremely important, notwithstanding that there has been a solid payment history. And, equally important to consider with existing customers is what your credit exposure is to each on a percentage of your portfolio. For example, if the financing for a particular customer is more than a few percent of your financing portfolio once your operation gets going, you might want to cap what you are willing to finance for that particular customer. And, in this case, you can consider selling off one or more transactions, or financing the receivables for one or more particular transactions by borrowing on a nonrecourse basis the funding necessary to finance a particular customer, to keep your credit exposure to a particular customer within manageable limits. In any event, there are many ways to manage your financed portfolio, all of which should be kept in mind.

Determine What Basic Types of Financing Will be Offered

As suggested earlier, depending on the products you are offering, consideration should be given to what type of financing to offer, such as lease financing, a rental arrangement (which can be the same as a lease arrangement with merely the document name changed), a conditional sale arrangement, a managed services arrangement, a fee-per-use arrangement, or some hybrid form of contract arrangement, the latter three of which may need some form of support from your company if the financing is to be debt financed by, or sold to, a third-party financing company, as discussed in Chapter 3. The basic document concepts are explained in Chapter 9. Typically, as already stated, offering basic lease and conditional sale financing is a good financing base to start with.

Develop a Customer Account Administration Process

An important part of setting up an in-house financing activity is to decide how the administration of the financings will be handled, including state tax compliance and payment processing and contract payment billing and collection.

Billing, Collection, and Tax Administration: In-House or Third Party

In the past, third-party and bank-affiliated leasing companies have staffed, at a substantial cost, the internal administration of their financial contracts, including contract payment billing and collection and monitoring and paying applicable state and any local taxes, such as sales and use (rent) taxes, all of which for a large financing activity required a substantial number of employees and expensive software. In the very recent years, however, because of available third-party support services, many financing companies are now actively considering streamlining their *back-office* operations by outsourcing some or all of their administration process to companies that now specialize in providing transaction billing, collection, and portfolio report generation, such as Great America Financial Services (www.greatamerica.com). The state tax administration, a critical aspect of financing customers, can also be outsourced to companies specialized in handling state and local tax matters, such as Vertex, Inc. (www.vertexinc.com). All of this streamlining not only cuts costs, but can also substantially simplify the entire financing process.

Determine What Reports are a Must and What Additional Reports You Want

Regardless of how the administration of your financing contracts is handled, a decision must be made as to what finance transaction-related reports you will need. At a bare minimum, you should have reports that track finance contract payments made and payment delinquencies, which should be run monthly, or bi-monthly. At times, incorrect billing information can cause an account to become delinquent at the start, something that should be corrected as soon as discovered. It is also advisable, even if all billing and collection aspects are handled by a qualified third party, to hire an individual to monitor reports to ensure collections are being timely received and who is able to proactively take any immediate necessary collection action in addition to that assumed by a third-party service provider when payment delays are extensive. And, someone who is also able to coordinate, as necessary, the hiring of experienced outside collection counsel or a collection agency to support the collection activity. If you do not have any way to identify recommended collection counsel, a search by state at https://martindale.com is a place to start. Additionally, worth considering is a report showing the monthly product sales and financing progress and, if there are multiple sales personnel, the financing status of each financing allocated by individual sales personnel.

Consider Fully Automating Your Processes

Customer Credit Applications

As already suggested, any credit application process should be available online and automated, through any processing software acquired, allowing each customer to confidentially enter credit data into an online application. Online access to a credit application is best set up using available third-party software designed for leasing and financing operations, such as, for example, the software offered by Terra Vista Software, referenced in Chapter 1. Alternatively, the software should also permit your product sales representative to enter customer credit information needed for processing. Finally, any acquired financing processing software should, if the credit assessment is acceptable, result in the automatic issuance of an approval, and if not met, automatically notify your credit manager so that an individual assessment can be made.

Structuring Offers

Any financing processing software you, as a product vendor, acquire should permit a selection of various financing products offered, such as a lease or a conditional sale, as well as various financing periods for each financing product. And, once a form of financing and period is selected, the actual dollar periodic payment amounts should be displayed. Doing this by hand for every potential transaction is time consuming and will unnecessarily delay your financing process.

Your Customer Information Should be Automatically Inserted into Your Credit Approval

Your financing processing software should, if your credit conditions are met, automatically populate and electronically deliver a credit approval to whoever you decide to select in advance, either to the customer directly or to your sales individual for personal delivery to your customer.

The Finance Documentation

Once a firm financing offer is accepted by a customer, something that should be capable of being done electronically online, your processing software should automatically populate the applicable financing contract and related documents that should have been uploaded into your financing processing software with the relevant customer information that has been entered into the software system, such as type of financing and the financing period chosen, as well as the customer's name and address, for delivery either directly to the customer or your sales individual for personal delivery to your customer.

Management Oversight

As mentioned earlier, financing contract management reports should be generated by internal software or by a third-party service provider you are using on at least a monthly basis, showing the status of billing and collection activity.

Security Interest and Creditor Lien Filings

As part of any in-house financing operation, you should contract with a lien filing service to file necessary liens or other security interests-type (Uniform Commercial Code) filings, discussed in Chapter 13. Companies such as Cogency Global Inc. (https://cogencyglobal.com/) offer this type of service at a reasonable cost.

Monitor First Payments to Minimize Collection Issues

It is not unusual for transaction contract billing to be set up incorrectly at the start, particularly when deals are under 250,000 U.S. dollars. Accordingly, you should carefully monitor the receipt of the first payment following your initial invoicing through your required reports, as suggested earlier in this chapter. Doing so will give you the opportunity to make any necessary adjustments quickly. For example, it is not unusual for a payment invoice to be sent in the case of a large company to the incorrect individual or payment department and, as a result, not have the payment processed, something that will typically occur in connection with your first payment invoice. Immediately calling the company and determining the correct individual will prevent continuing payment delays.

The Economics of Collecting Payments from a Nonpaying Customer

The difficulty reality is that even if you have legally tight financing contracts that are clearly enforceable in a court action, the cost of taking any collection action must be evaluated when there is a financing contract nonpayment or other default. That is, it is may be better to simply write the contract off as a loss rather than spending additional money to take collection action, all of which will depend on the dollar amount still due you. For example, spending 10,000 U.S. dollars to institute legal action on a 5,000 U.S. dollar delinquent account would not be cost-effective, but it would be on a 200,000 U.S. dollar delinquent account.

Using Outside Collection Counsel

When a customer account becomes delinquent, you will need to decide the most cost-effective way of resolving the issue. If considerable effort and time have been invested by, say, an in-house collection individual in addition to any third-party back-office service provider without resolution, then you will need another option. Hiring outside legal collection counsel is one possibility, but that should be assessed considering the amount that is due. For example, as stated earlier, if there is an outstanding payment of, say, 5,000 to 10,000 U.S. dollars, then, unless the collection is well assured, the customer is financially solvent, and the financing contract is well drafted, any cost for counsel can quickly further erode profits, even if the outstanding balance is collected. It is not unusual, if outside counsel files a collection lawsuit, for legal costs to quickly rise to 5,000 to 10,000 U.S. dollars and much higher today. That may be acceptable for a multi-million-dollar transaction, but not for a 10,000 to 20,000 U.S. dollar transaction. And, if the legal collection efforts are not successful, that further increases the loss. Even if legal counsel is successful, the amount collected will typically be offset by legal fees, if their legal fees cost cannot be collected from the defaulting customer. So, in all cases, a business assessment must be made whether to use outside counsel, and, if used, the resulting cost incurred should be carefully monitored. Very simply, filing a lawsuit should be the last resort.

Using a Collection Agency

Hiring a collection agency that works on a percentage of amounts collected basis is another possible approach, at times less expensive than hiring outside legal counsel. But, here, an in-house collection manager or a good third-party back-office service provider can serve the same function for, possibly, in the case of an outside provider, a flat engagement fee.

Develop a Product Re-Marketing Strategy

As suggested in Chapter 2, one of the key profit strategies for many third-party leasing companies, and one that should also be considered by a product vendor with a financing operation, whether fully in-house or using a third-party vendor program, is to develop a secondary market operation for used products coming off lease contracts. In the case of a financing activity set up with a third-party vendor program, of course, this is only applicable if you enter into a product re-marketing arrangement with the third-party financing company where you will handle product re-marketing for a share in re-marketing proceeds. In either case, set up properly, this can be a highly profitable activity. So, you, as a product vendor, are well advised to consider how to develop a secondary market of used product returned at the end-of-lease contracts or in the case of any financing contract customer default if one has not already been developed internally.

Hiring Financing Operation Consultants

There should be no doubt that a product vendor intending to set up an in-house financing operation, if the necessary expertise is unavailable internally, should consider hiring leasing and financing consultants who can bring necessary experienced guidance and information. The credit operation, as you now know, as well as the legal considerations, are key to the startup and ongoing success of an in-house financing operation. In looking for a consultant, it is best to identify one who, in fact, has practical business experience in the area in which you will need advice. For example, a good choice for a business consultant is one who has more than a theoretical financial background, and the same is true for legal counsel. In the case of an attorney, you want someone who is not an ivory tower practitioner, but one who has been intimately involved in business aspects of financing, and possibly someone who has worked in other startup situations. For example, you want to avoid creating financing documents that will be too overpowering or complex or having credit evaluations devoid of common sense considerations. There is no substitute for being able to assess and accept minor or inconsequential risks that might not be recommended by someone solely with a theoretical background.

Summary

A product vendor deciding to set up an in-house financing operation should develop a checklist of what items will be needed to accomplish using outside consultants and then, consider what aspects can be handled by existing internal resources. Taking advantage of the many available outside resources to handle aspects, such as contract administration, that cannot be done economically or at all internally will make the process of setting up a fully functional, in-house financing operation both manageable and cost-effective.

CHAPTER 7

Financial Analysis of Leases and Other Product Financings

Overview

As you now know, there are many factors a product vendor needs to consider in deciding whether to enter into an equipment lease or other financing contract, but the financial aspect is one of the most important considerations. The financial considerations are also important for a prospective lessee or borrower and, accordingly, a product vendor should have a basic understanding, provided as follows, of both what is important to their financial investment outlay and how a savvy customer should do their lease or borrowing analysis.

The Importance of Cash Flow and Timing for a Prospective Lessee or Borrower

In making a financial assessment of whether to lease or buy equipment with internal or borrowed funds, a prospective lessee must take the varying cash flows, and their timing, into account for each alternative. Stated simply, how much are the cash inflows and outflows, and when do they occur? The timing of the cash inflows and outflows is critical because of the principle—referred to as the time value of money—that the money received earlier is worth more than the money received later.

The following example illustrates very simplistically how taking cash flow and its timing into account alters the result of an analysis.

Illustrative example: Cash flow and time value: An equipment user is considering two options: leasing equipment over a seven-year period with an annual rent of 990 U.S. dollars payable at the beginning of each year and buying the equipment using a seven-year loan with 1,000 U.S. dollars annual payments due at each year's end. By choosing to lease, the company would pay out 990 U.S. dollars one year earlier than it would have to pay the required 1,000 U.S. dollars loan payment. If the company could earn, say, 6% a year after taxes on its available funds, giving up the 990 U.S. dollars in advance would result in a *loss* of 59.40 U.S. dollars (6% × $990 = $59.40) the first year. In this case, the advance payment could be said to cost 1,049.40 U.S. dollars ($990 + $59.40 = $1,049.40). Putting other considerations aside, the 1,000 U.S. dollars loan payment would have been less expensive. If the company were able to earn only 1% a year after taxes, paying the 990 U.S. dollars would result in only a 9.90 U.S. dollars *loss* (1% × $990 = $9.90). That is, the effective cost of paying the 990 U.S. dollars would have been 999.90 U.S. dollars, instead of 1,049.40 U.S. dollars. In the latter case, the 1,000 U.S. dollars loan payment could be said to be more expensive.

The Prospective Lessee's Analysis

Once a company has decided it needs certain equipment, it must determine how to finance its acquisition. The following discussion will address three alternatives:

- The user leases the equipment (the leasing alternative)
- The user draws on their general funds to buy the equipment (the purchase alternative)
- The user takes out a specific loan to buy the equipment (the financing alternative)

This section will compare those three financial alternatives by using a common method for taking cash flows and their timing into account, sometimes referred to as the discounted cash flow—or present value—analysis method. The first step will be to compute the periodic costs and tax savings for each alternative. The next step will be to factor in the timing of those cash flows so that there is a basis for comparison by calculating the present value of each alternative's cash flows. To compute the present value of a series of future cash flows, an interest rate—referred to as the discount rate—must be selected to discount the flows back to their present worth. The result will be the present value cost of the alternatives. Because getting to these results involves many computations, the following analysis will center around one hypothetical equipment acquisition situation.

> **Note:** The financial analysis computations from which the examples in this chapter were developed were done on SuperTRUMP, a lease analysis computer software program, developed and offered by Ivory Consulting Corporation (www.ivorycc.com). The information from the computer analysis results was at times summarized by the author to aid in the explanation of the concepts described in the text material.

A Typical Equipment User's Financial Alternatives

White Industries wants to acquire a new high-end computer system and can use all available tax benefits. White is considering three financing alternatives—the lease alternative, the purchase alternative, and the financing alternative. Additional facts include (assumed for ease of illustration without regard to whether any applicable tax or other rules will be satisfied) the following:

General data

Computer system cost	One million U.S. dollars
Depreciable period	Five years
Residual value	0 U.S. dollar
Investment tax credit	$0%
Accounting basis	Accrual
White Industries combined income tax rate (Federal, state, and local)	35%
White Industries tax year	Calendar year
Delivery date	January 1, 2019
Depreciation method	MACRS (Half-Year, DB/SL 200%)

Proposed financial lease

Lease term	Seven years
Rental payments	200,000 U.S. dollars, payable in seven annual payments in arrears
Lease simple interest rate	9.1961%
Commencement date	January 1, 2019

Proposed bank loan

Loan amount	One million U.S. dollars, repayable in seven equal annual payments of 205,405.50 U.S. dollars in arrears
Loan term	Seven years
Long term interest rate	10.0%
Commencement date	January 1, 2019

The Cost of the Leasing Alternative

The first step is to compute the after-tax cost of the various alternatives. Table 7.1 sets out those costs for the leasing alternative.

Table 7.1

Year ending	Rental payments	Tax savings from rent deductions	After-tax cost	Cumulative after-tax cost
December 30, 2019	$ 0.00	$70,000	$(70,000)	$(70,000)
December 30, 2020	200,000	70,000	130,000	60,000
December 30, 2021	200,000	70,000	130,000	190,000
December 30, 2022	200,000	70,000	130,000	320,000
December 30, 2023	200,000	70,000	130,000	450,000
December 30, 2024	200,000	70,000	130,000	580,000
December 30, 2025	200,000	70,000	130,000	710,000
December 30, 2026	200,000	0	200,000	910,000
Total	$1,400,000	$490,000	$910,000	N/A

Table 7.1 is computed as follows:

- The Rental payments are the annual payments the lessee must make. These begin in 2020 because the rent is payable annually in arrears.

- The Tax savings from rent deductions represents the income tax savings White Industries would realize from the rent deductions, computed at White Industries' assumed combined 35% bracket (federal, state, and local).
- The After-tax cost is derived by subtracting the Tax savings from the rent deductions from the Rental payments.
- The Cumulative after-tax cost represents the transaction's total after-tax cost as of each year end.

The result is a total after-tax cost of 910,000 U.S. dollars, if White Industries leases the computer system.

The Cost of the Purchase Alternative

The next step is to compute the after-tax cost of an outright purchase using internal funds. The Annual depreciation expense indicated in Table 7.2 is the amount White Industries would be entitled to deduct under MACRS depreciation as the computer owner over a five-year period. The other columns are computed as in the leasing example (Table 7.1):

Table 7.2

Year ending	Equity	Annual depreciation expense	Tax savings	After-tax cost	Cumulative after-tax
December 30, 2019	$1,000,000	$200,000	$ 70,000	$930,000	$930,000
December 30, 2020	0	320,000	112,000	(112,000)	818,000
December 30, 2021	0	192,000	67,200	(67,200)	750,800
December 30, 2022	0	115,200	40,320	(40,320)	710,480
December 30, 2023	0	115,200	40,320	(40,320)	670,160
December 30, 2024	0	57,600	20,160	(20,160)	650,000
Total	$1,000,000	$1,000,000	$350,000	$650,000	N/A

Comparing Cash Flows

Thus, at this point in the analysis, the purchase alternative seems substantially less expensive than the lease alternatives as its total after-tax cost is only 650,000 U.S. dollars compared with 910,000 U.S. dollars for leasing. However, this ignores the leasing cash flow advantage because, as shown in Table 7.3, the total cost of the lease is less until the seventh year.

Table 7.3 Cash flow comparison

Year	Lease cumulative after-tax cost	Purchase cumulative after-tax cost	Lease cash advantage
2019	$(70,000)	$930,000	$1,000,000
2020	60,000	818,000	758,000
2021	190,000	750,000	560,000
2022	320,000	710,000	390,000
2023	450,000	670,000	220,000
2024	580,000	650,000	70,000
2025	710,000	650,000	(60,000)
2026	910,000	650,000	(260,000)

Plainly, leasing does conserve money in the early years, and those available funds could be put to use elsewhere. The resulting earnings on those funds would offset the disparity in total cost between the two alternatives. Thus, it cannot be concluded that leasing is more expensive until the present value of the two alternative cash flows is compared.

To calculate the present value of the leasing and buying cash flows, White Industries must discount both alternatives' cash flows to their present worth. Choosing a 10% annual discount rate and assuming White Industries pays its estimated taxes on April 15, June 15, September 15, and December 15 of each year, the after-tax cash flows for the leasing and purchase alternatives are in Table 7.4 as follows:

Table 7.4 Present value comparison

Year	Lease		Purchase	
	After-tax cost	Present value	After-tax cost	Present value
January 01, 2019	0.00	0.00	1,000,000.00	1,000,000.00
April 15, 2019	(17,500.00)	(17,008.64)	(17,500.00)	(17,008.64)
June 15, 2019	(17,500.00)	(16,729.81)	(17,500.00)	(16,729.81)
September 15, 2019	(17,500.00)	(16,321.77)	(17,500.00)	(16,321.77)
December 15, 2019	(17,500.00)	(15,923.67)	(17,500.00)	(15,923.67)
	70,000.00	65,983.89	930,000.00	934,016.11
January 01, 2020	200,000.00	181,179.00	0.00	0.00
April 15, 2020	(17,500.00)	(15,408.09)	(28,000.00)	(24,852.95)
June 15, 2020	(17,500.00)	(15,166.50)	(28,000.00)	(24,245.80)
September 15, 2020	(17,500.00)	(14,785.85)	(28,000.00)	(23,657.37)
December 15, 2020	(17,500.00)	(14,425.22)	(28,000.00)	(23,080.38)
	130,000.00	121,404.92	112,000.00	95,639.47
January 01, 2021	200,00.00	164,130.23	0.00	0.00
April 15, 2021	(17,500.00)	(13,958.16)	(16,800.00)	(13,399.83)
June 15, 2021	(17,500.00)	(13,729.34)	(16,800.00)	(13,180.16)
September 15, 2021	(17,500.00)	(13,394.47)	(16,800.00)	(12,858.70)
December 15, 2021	(17,500.00)	(13,067.78)	(16,800.00)	(12,545.07)
	130,000.00	109,980.48	67,200.00	51,983.76
January 01, 2022	200,000.00	148,685.24	0.00	0.00
April 15, 2022	(17,500.00)	(12,644.67)	(10,080.00)	(7,283.33)
June 15, 2022	(17,500.00)	(12,437.38)	(10,080.00)	(7,163.93)
September 15, 2022	(17,500.00)	(12,134.03)	(10,080.00)	(8,989.20)
December 15, 2022	(17,500.00)	(11,838.08)	(10,080.00)	(8,818.737)
	130,000.00	99,631.08	40,320.00	28,255.19
January 01, 2023	200,000.00	134,693.66	0.00	0.00
April 15, 2023	(17,500.00)	(11,454.78)	(10,080.00)	(6,597.95)
June 15, 2023	(17,500.00)	(11,267.00)	(10,080.00)	(6,459.79)
September 15, 2023	(17,500.00)	(10,992.19)	(10,080.00)	(6,331.50)
December 15, 2023	(17,500.00)	(10,724.09)	(10,080.00)	(6,177.08)
	130,000.00	90,255.60	40,320.00	25,598.32

(*Continued*)

Table 7.4 Present value comparison (Continued)

Year	Lease After-tax cost	Lease Present value	Purchase After-tax cost	Purchase Present value
January 01, 2024	200,000.00	122,018.71	0.00	0.00
April 15, 2024	(17,500.00)	(10,376.86)	(5,040.00)	(2,988.54)
June 15, 2024	(17,500.00)	(10,206.75)	(5,040.00)	(2,939.54)
September 15, 2024	(17,500.00)	(9,957.80)	(5,040.00)	(2,867.85)
December 15, 2024	(17,500.00)	(9,714.93)	(5,040.00)	(2,797.90)
	130,000.00	81,762.37	20,160.00	11,593.83
January 01, 2025	200,000.00	110,536.50	0.00	0.00
April 15, 2025	(17,500.00)	(9,400.38)	0.00	0.00
June 15, 2025	(17,500.00)	(9,246.27)	0.00	0.00
September 15, 2025	(17,500.00)	(9,020.75)	0.00	0.00
December 15, 2025	(17,500.00)	(8,800.74)	0.00	0.00
	130,000.00	74,068.36	0.00	0.00
January 01, 2026	200,000.00	100,134.79	0.00	0.00
	200,000.00	100,134.79	0.00	0.00
Total	910,000	611,253.72	650,000.00	720,947.55

The discounted cash flow analysis clearly reverses the outcome. The leasing alternative's present worth is 611,253.72 U.S. dollars, while the purchase alternative's is 720,947.55 U.S. dollars. Based on this analysis, leasing the computer system would be less expensive than buying with internal funds.

The Financing Alternative

The next step is to calculate the financing alternative's cash flow in the same manner. The computation is the same as the purchase alternative (Table 7.2) with the additional factors being the payment of the 10.0% interest and the tax savings on deducting the interest. The after-tax cost calculations are in Table 7.5 as follows:

Table 7.5

Year ending	Debt payments	Year-end principal balance outstanding	10.0% interest on principal	Tax savings (depreci- ation and interest)	Net after- tax cost
December 30, 2019	$ 0.00	$1,000,000.00	$100,000.000	$105,000.00	$(105,000.00)
December 30, 2020	205,405.50	894,594.50	89,459.45	143,310.81	62,094.69
December 30, 2021	205,405.50	778,645.45	77,846.85	94,452.70	110,952.80
December 30, 2022	205,405.50	651,107.80	65,110.78	63,108.77	142,296.73
December 30, 2023	205,405.50	510,813.08	51,081.31	58,198.46	147,207.04
December 30, 2024	205,405.50	356,488.88	35,648.89	32,637.11	172,768.39
December 30, 2025	205,405.50	186,732.27	18,673.23	6,535.63	198,869.87
December 30, 2026	205,405.50	0.00	0.00	0.00	205,405.02
Total	$1,437,838.50	$0.00	$437,838.50	$503,243.47	$934,595.02

The present worth calculation, again using a 10% discount rate, results in the following (again assuming estimated all income tax payments are made on April 15, June 15, September 15, and December 15 of each tax year):

Table 7.6 Present value comparison

Year	Lease After-tax cost	Lease Present value	Financing After-tax cost	Financing Present value
January 01, 2019	0.00	0.00	0.00	0.00
April 15, 2019	(17,500.00)	(17,008.64)	(26,250.00)	(25,512.96)
June 15, 2019	(17,500.00)	(16,729.81)	(26,250.00)	(25,094.71)
September 15, 2019	(17,500.00)	(16,321.77)	(26,250.00)	(24,482.65)

(Continued)

Table 7.6 Present value comparison (Continued)

Year	Lease		Financing	
	After-tax cost	Present value	After-tax cost	Present value
December 15, 2019	(17,500.00)	(15,923.67)	(26,250.00)	(23,885.51)
	70,000.00	65,983.89	105,000.00	98,975.83
January 01, 2020	200,000.00	181,179.00	205,405.50	186,076.43
April 15, 2020	(17,500.00)	(15,408.09)	(35,827.70)	(31,544.94)
June 15, 2020	(17,500.00)	(15,166.50)	(35,827.70)	(31,027.81)
September 15, 2020	(17,500.00)	(14,785.85)	(35,827.70)	(30,271.04)
December 15, 2020	(17,500.00)	(14,425.22)	(35,827.70)	(29,532.72)
	130,000.00	121,404.92	62,094.69	63,699.91
January 01, 2021	200,00.00	164,130.23	205,405.50	168,566.26
April 15, 2021	(17,500.00)	(13,958.16)	(23,613.17)	(18,834.08)
June 15, 2021	(17,500.00)	(13,729.34)	(23,613.17)	(18,525.33)
September 15, 2021	(17,500.00)	(13,394.47)	(23,613.17)	(18,073.49)
December 15, 2021	(17,500.00)	(13,067.78)	(23,613.17)	(17,632.67)
	130,000.00	109,980.48	110,952.80	95,500.68
January 01, 2022	200,000.00	148,685.24	205,405.50	152,703.83
April 15, 2022	(17,500.00)	(12,644.67)	(15,777.19)	(11,399.85)
June 15, 2022	(17,500.00)	(12,437.38)	(15,777.19)	(11,212.97)
September 15, 2022	(17,500.00)	(12,134.03)	(15,777.19)	(10,939.48)
December 15, 2022	(17,500.00)	(11,838.08)	(15,777.19)	(10,672.66)
	130,000.00	99,631.08	142,296.73	108,478.87
January 01, 2023	200,000.00	134,693.66	205,405.50	138,334.09
April 15, 2023	(17,500.00)	(11,454.78)	(14,549.61)	(9,523.58)
June 15, 2023	(17,500.00)	(11,267.00)	(14,549.61)	(9,367.45)
September 15, 2023	(17,500.00)	(10,992.19)	(14,549.61)	(9,138.98)
December 15, 2023	(17,500.00)	(10,724.09)	(14,549.61)	(8,916.08)
	130,000.00	90,255.60	147,207.04	101,388.00
January 01, 2024	200,000.00	122,018.71	205,405.00	125,316.57
April 15, 2024	(17,500.00)	(10,376.86)	(8,159.28)	(4,838.15)
June 15, 2024	(17,500.00)	(10,206.75)	(8,159.28)	(4,758.84)
September 15, 2024	(17,500.00)	(9,957.80)	(8,159.28)	(4,642.77)
December 15, 2024	(17,500.00)	(9,714.93)	(8,159.28)	(4,529.53)
	130,000.00	81,762.37	172,768.39	106,547.27
January 01, 2025	200,000.00	110,536.50	205,405.50	113,524.03

April 15, 2025	(17,500.00)	(9,400.38)	(1,633.91)	(877.68)
June 15, 2025	(17,500.00)	(9,246.27)	(1,633.91)	(863.29)
September 15, 2025	(17,500.00)	(9,020.75)	(1,633.91)	(842.23)
December 15, 2025	(17,500.00)	(8,800.74)	(1,633.91)	(821.69)
	130,000.00	74,068.36	198,869.87	110,119.14
January 01, 2026	200,000.00	100,134.79	205,405.50	102,841.18
	200,000.00	100,134.79	205,405.50	102,841.18
Total	910,000	611,253.72	934,595.02	589,599.23

Comparing Cash Flows

As Table 7.6 shows, the financial alternative results in a present value cost of (598,599.23 U.S. dollars), the least expensive of the three alternatives. This result is not intended to mean that financing with borrowed funds is always the best alternative because the specific result was based on the assumed facts. Rather, it is intended to show how dramatically the present value cash flow analysis alters the result. The financing alternative, with the highest cumulative cost, results in the lowest present worth cost, and the purchase alternative, with the lowest cumulative cost, results in the highest present worth cost.

The Lessor's Lease Investment Analysis

A prospective lessor, in making its financial analysis, needs to determine what its economic return will be on the leased equipment. The concepts of cash flow and present value also play an important part in the lessor's analysis.

This section will analyze one type of lease, the non-leveraged lease, where the lessor uses their own funds entirely to buy the equipment.

Non-Leveraged Lease

As explained earlier, in a non-leveraged lease, the lessor supplies all the money necessary to buy the equipment from their own funds. Whether this type of investment will make economic sense depends on how profitable the transaction will be to the lessor. Thus, determining the profit—commonly referred to as the rate of return (usually computed on an after-tax basis)—is a threshold issue in any financial lease investment evaluation.

Traditionally, an after-tax lessor's rate of return has been defined as the interest rate—sometimes referred to as the discount rate—that will discount a lease's after-tax cash flows back to a value equal to its initial cash outlay. Or, looking at it another way, it is the rate that, when applied to the original cash investment, will produce the future cash flow amounts generated by the lease.

To explain the investor rate of return analysis approach, we will work through a hypothetical non-leveraged lease example, assuming the following facts:

Equipment data

Cost	One million U.S. dollars
Depreciable life	Five years
Residual value	0 U.S. dollars
Delivery date	January 1, 2019
Lease commencement date	January 1, 2019
Description	Computer system

Lease investment data

Lease term	Seven years
Rental payments	Seven annual payments in arrears, each equal to 200,000 U.S. dollars
ITC	0%
Lessor combined income tax rate (Federal, state, and local)	35%
Depreciation method	MACRS (Half-Year, DB/SL 200)

Based on those facts, and the assumption that the lessor is an accrual basis taxpayer, Table 7.7 sets out the lessor's cash flow and federal income reports.

Table 7.7

Year ending	Rent income	Annual depreciation	Taxable income	Total taxes paid	Equity	Pre-tax cash flow	After-tax cash flow
December 30, 2019	0.00	200,000.00	0.00	0.00	1,000,000.00	(1,000,000.00)	(1,000,000.00)
December 30. 2020	200,000.00	320,000.00	(120,000.00)	(42,000.00)	0.00	200,000.00	242,000.00
December 30, 2021	200,000.00	192,000.00	8,000.00	2,800.00	0.00	200,000.00	197,200.00
December30, 2022	200,000.00	115,200.00	84,800.00	29,680.00	0.00	200,000.00	170,320.00
December 30, 2023	200,000.00	115,200.00	84,800.00	29,680.00	0.00	200,000.00	170,320.00
December 30, 2024	200,000.00	57,600.00	142,400.00	49,840.00	0.00	200,000.00	150,160.00
December 30, 2025	200,000.00	0.00	200,000.00	70,000.00	0.00	200,000.00	130,000.00
December 30, 2026	200,000.00	0.00	0.00	0.00	0.00	200,000.00	200,000.00
Total	$1,400,000.00	$1,000,000.00	$400,000.00	$140,000.00	$1,000,000.00	$400,000.00	$260,000.00

The columns in Table 7.7 are computed as follows:

Annual depreciation represents the amount of the annual MACRS deduction available to the lessor on the computer as five-year recovery property and applying the half-year convention (all discussed in Chapter 11).

The Taxable income is the result of subtracting the annual depreciation deduction from the rent income. The lessor is an accrual basis taxpayer, so the rent income is accrued for the year ending December 30, 2019, for income tax purposes, resulting in no taxable income for this year (200,000 U.S. dollars rent income - 200,000 U.S. dollars depreciation expense = 0), and there would be no tax accrued rent income for the year ending December 30, 2026.

The Total taxes paid represents the dollar savings or cost on the income or loss in the Taxable income column based on a 35% combined income tax rate (federal, state, and local). Where the figure is negative, the lessor reduces their overall tax liability by that amount.

The After-tax cash flow results from adjusting the Pre-tax cash flow by the amount of the taxes paid or saved. Thus, where the Total taxes paid figure is negative, this amount is added to the Pre-tax cash flow; where the Total taxes paid figure is positive, this amount is subtracted from the Pre-tax cash flow.

Once the after-tax cash flows have been calculated, the after-tax rate of return—often referred to as the after-tax yield—can be found by finding the interest rate that will discount the after-tax cash flows back to the cost of the computer, one million U.S. dollars. Here, the lessor will receive an after-tax yield equal to 9.1961%.

Summary

The key to a proper lessee lease versus purchase analysis, or a lessors' investment return analysis, is determining the various cash inflows and outflows on a present value basis. Because of the complexity of making these determinations, and the risk of human computation error, it is always advisable to use one of the many computer programs available today for these purposes.

CHAPTER 8

Understanding the Lease Accounting Rules

Background

During the early years of the equipment leasing business, the accounting profession devoted considerable time and effort discussing how leases should be accounted for, both from the standpoint of the lessor and the lessee. There were many inconsistencies and substantive disagreements. Today, the subject of accounting for leases has been addressed by the accounting profession's standard-setting body, the Financial Accounting Standards Board (FASB), as set forth the *Statement of Financial Accounting Standards No. 13-Accounting for Leases*, in effect since 1977. Commonly referred to as FAS No. 13, the rules promulgated established the standards to be followed by lessors and lessees in accounting for and reporting lease transactions.

Since FAS No. 13 was issued, the FASB had been called on to address a wide variety of issues raised by FAS 13, and various amendments and interpretations have been issued to clarify or handle many of the guideline's complex issues. Some of the newly issued amendments and interpretations significantly impact lessees. For example, under the original FASB-promulgated lease accounting rules, some lease transactions, referred to as *operating leases*, or leases that typically were not *full payout* in nature, essentially those in which all or substantially all of the equipment cost was not paid through lease rents, could be treated as *off-balance* sheet transactions by lessees for accounting purposes. That is, if the lease was classified for accounting purposes as an operating, as opposed to a capital (now called a *finance*) lease, discussed in the following material, it did not have to be reported in the lessee's financial statements as a long-term liability, and the rents could be expensed as they occurred (in effect, off-balance sheet treatment), thereby minimizing the effect of the transaction on key financial ratios that may impact the lessee's cost of future funds. One of the significant benefits of the off-balance sheet treatment was that a long-term lease, at times, could be used to obtain needed equipment without violating covenants in loan and credit agreements that restricted the amount of long-term indebtedness a lessee may incur. This is essentially no longer possible.

One important point for the reader to be aware of is that the technical aspects of lease accounting are very complex and nuanced for both a lessor and a lessee, and the explanation in this chapter is meant only to provide a general understanding of the accounting rules.

Understanding Lessee Lease Accounting Classifications

Under FAS No. 13, today a lessee must account for and report a lease in their financial statements as either a *finance* (formerly referred to as a *capital*) lease or an *operating* lease, depending on how the transaction is structured. In certain cases, it may not be advisable for a company to lease equipment because of the accounting treatment impact.

A lease must be treated by a lessee as a finance lease under FAS No.13 if, at its inception, it meets one or more of the following criteria: (i) it provides for a transfer of the property's ownership to the lessee at the end of the lease term, (ii) the lease contains a bargain purchase option, (iii) the lease term is equal to or greater than 75 percent of the property's estimated economic useful life, or (iv) the present value (using, typically, the lessee's incremental borrowing rate) of the *minimum lease payments* at the lease inception is equal to or greater than 90 percent of the excess of the fair value of the leased property (determined at the beginning of the lease). If the lease does not meet any of the above criteria, it is classified as an operating lease. *Minimum lease payments* include the minimum lease term rental payments stated in the lease and any lessee guarantee of the residual value of the leased equipment at the end of the lease term, whether or not the lessee payment of the guarantee is a purchase of the leased equipment.

An operating lease is like a rental contract, with the lessee reporting the lease payments as operating expenses, but not claiming any depreciation expense. The lessor (the equipment owner), however, can claim the depreciation tax benefits. Finance leases, on the other hand, are viewed like a financed purchase—in other words, under the lease terms, the lessee may have some of the benefits of ownership, such as charging depreciation expense, and accounting for the asset on the balance sheet as a capital asset.

The Impact on a Lessee of the Lease Accounting Requirements

If a lease is classified as a finance lease, the lessee does not state the rent as an expense item. The lessee must record the lease as an asset and an obligation at an amount equal to the present value (determined as of the beginning of the lease term) of the minimum lease payments during the lease term. *Nonlease components*, payments due under the lease for goods or services separate from the property leased, included in the payments, such as insurance, maintenance, and taxes, that the lessor must pay (passed through costs billed to the lessee) must be included before making the present value computation. If the present value of the minimum lease payments is greater than the property's *fair value* (generally its purchase cost) determined at the beginning of the lease, then the fair value is to be recorded.

A finance lease must be written off (amortized) by a lessee under certain specific rules, dictated by which of the four finance lease classification criteria are met. If the lease meets the first or second criterion (i.e., property ownership is transferred to the lessee at lease end or the lessee has a bargain purchase option), the lessee must write it off in a manner consistent with the usual depreciation practice for assets they own. If the lease does not meet either of these two criteria, the lessee must amortize the property over a period equal to the lease term in a manner consistent with its normal depreciation practice down to a value it expects the property to be worth at the end of the lease. In other words, a lease characterized as a finance (non-operating) lease, for lease accounting purposes in effect is to be reported in the lessee's financial statements as though it basically had bought the equipment and taken out a loan to finance its purchase.

For leases categorized as operating leases, prior to the new changes to the original FASB accounting rules, generally, the rental payments could be charged to expense as they become due on a straight-line basis, whether or not they were, in fact, payable on a straight-line basis. They were treated as off-balance sheet items. Under the recently revised FASB lease accounting rules, which were 10 years in the making, and are now effective for public business entities beginning on January 1, 2019, and for all other entities beginning on January 1, 2020, operating leases, as stated earlier, can no longer qualify as an off-balance sheet item for lessees. That is, as of the applicable updated FAS 13 accounting rule effective dates, most operating lease obligations must be capitalized in the same manner as finance lease obligations and must be included as assets and as liabilities on the balance sheet, which affects some financial measurements, such as earnings before interest, taxes, depreciation, and amortization (commonly referred to as *EBITDA*), as well as operating leverage and interest coverage. Rent payments in the case of leases qualifying as operating leases can, however, be categorized as *non-debt*.

In certain situations, however, if a lease qualifies as a short-term lease, one that has a lease term of 12 months or less and does not have a purchase option the lessee is reasonably certain to exercise, it can be treated in a manner similar to how an operating lease had originally been treated as an off-balance sheet item, that is, not reflected on the lessee's balance sheet. All other leases, in effect, now become a balance sheet item, where the lessee must recognize the rent payments as a long-term liability, which must be amortized over the term of the lease.

It should also be kept in mind that equipment supplied under managed services and fee-per-use agreements, originally thought by some to be treated by customers/obligors as off-balance sheet obligations, may in fact, depending on the contract provisions, now require treatment similar to that required under traditional lease arrangements.

The Lease Classification Categories for a Lessor

For a lessor, FAS No. 13 now provides that all leases must be categorized as either sales-type leases, direct financing leases, or operating leases. A lease will be classified as a sales-type lease if the lease is classified as a finance lease for the lessee and is to be classified as a direct financing lease only if the lease is classified as a finance lease if, a result of a third-party end-of-lease residual guarantee, the present value of the minimum lease payments test is met. A lease is classified as an operating lease if it is not a direct financing lease or a sales-type lease.

Summary

The *Statement of Financial Accounting Standards No. 13-Accounting for Leases*, commonly referred to as FAS No. 13, sets forth the rules to be followed by lessors and lessees in accounting for and reporting lease transactions. FAS No. 13 in effect says that a lease that transfers substantially all of an asset's ownership benefits and risks to the lessee must be treated by the lessee in the same way as an asset bought with borrowed money is treated (finance lease treatment). The lessor must account for the lease as a sale or a financing. Operating lease obligations were originally not required by lessees to be recorded as balance sheet obligations, but, today, they must be capitalized in a manner similar to finance lease obligations. That is, they must be included as assets and as liabilities on the balance sheet. Rent payments in the case of leases qualifying as operating leases can, however, be categorized as *non-debt*. The rules can be complex, so care must be taken in assessing their impact on an equipment lease transaction.

CHAPTER 9

The Lease and Other Core Financing Documents

An Overview of What Financing Documents to Consider

Whether you decide to establish a fully functioning in-house financing operation or set up a third-party vendor program to provide customer product financing, you will need a set of form customer financing documents prior to starting your program. Invariably, if you decide to use a third-party vendor program, the financing company will have an existing set of forms that they typically use. However, that does not mean that you cannot review and modify their forms prior to the start of your arrangement to ensure that they are both customer-friendly and fit the type of financing you want to offer your customers. Most third-party financing companies offering vendor programs now use forms that are written in plain English, minimizing the often-complex legal terminology lawyers like to use.

The First Key Document: The Financing Proposal

In addition to deciding what financing contract forms to use, you should also develop a form of financing proposal, as suggested in Chapter 6, which could simply be a paragraph or two of the financing terms and conditions to be inserted in your product sales proposal or a standalone document. The proposal letter should outline the basic business financing *deal*. It does not have to cover every detail, but it should set the framework for the overall financing arrangement. In any event, you will want to ensure that you have addressed the following items applicable to your financing offer, either in the product sales proposal or in a separate financing proposal letter:

- The equipment configuration, including the number of equipment units involved
- The equipment's aggregate and per unit cost
- When the equipment delivery is anticipated
- The type of financing offered, that is, a lease, a conditional sale, or some other financing arrangement
- The financing term
- The rental or other payment periodicity, that is, monthly, quarterly, semi-annually, or annually—in advance or in arrears
- What options are available, such as renewal, upgrade, purchase, or early termination options
- The date by which the offer must be accepted
- The offer conditions that may apply, such as subject to internal credit review acceptability or mutually acceptable documentation

A proposal stage checklist has been included in the Appendix.

The Legal Status of a Proposal

A financing offer (proposal) is generally not legally enforceable by either party because of the conditions typically accompanying it, such as the offer stating that it is subject to an internal credit committee review and approval or mutually acceptable documentation, as well as any conditions that you or your customer may insert, such as approval by the customer's chief financial officer.

A *satisfactory documentation* condition in a financing proposal gives the parties a wide latitude to find justification to back out if they so desire. Simply, this condition leaves room for open-ended discussions on issues not even anticipated at the offering stage, such as whether the customer, in the case of a lease, offer should pay for the equipment's return to any lessor-designated location in the United States.

While an accepted written proposal may not be legally enforceable because of the stated conditions, it is important because the parties will invariably make a significant effort to complete the proposed transaction once agreed to, and it serves as a drafting guideline and reminder for the parties and their lawyers on the preliminary terms and conditions in negotiating the financing documents.

The Core Financing Contracts: An Overview

The most important financing document is the main contract, such as the lease or conditional sale agreement. Although a lease or other financing agreement can involve many complex, highly technical and, sometimes, overwhelming concepts, their central purpose is simple. For a lease, it is a contract in which a property owner, the lessor, transfers the right to use the property to another, the lessee, for a period of time. It will contain provisions that ensure the lessor's investment return, such as an unconditional payment obligation, which means the payments are not subject to cancelation. A sample equipment leasing agreement is included in the Appendix.

A conditional sale transaction, an outright sale for all cash, or a mortgage (purchase loan) differs from a lease. Under a conditional sale contract, the property owner providing the financing sells the property, not merely its use, to the buyer. Typically, the conditional sale financing party retains the technical legal title to the property until the buyer performs certain conditions, usually the full payment of the purchase price in installments, at which time, the legal title is automatically transferred to the buyer.

In a mortgage contract, a buyer of a property borrows from a third-party lender some or all the money necessary to buy the property. The lender, or mortgagee, as security for the repayment of its loan, requires the borrower, or mortgagor, to give them a security interest in (lien on) the property. The borrower has possession of, and title to, the property, subject to the lender's right to foreclose on, and take control over, the property in the event of a loan default.

In an outright sale contract arrangement, the property owner unconditionally transfers the property, including the title, to the buyer and, at the same time, the buyer pays the seller the full purchase price.

Managed services and fee-per-use agreements, discussed in Chapter 14, are often custom forms designed to provide the services provider's terms and conditions, which typically include providing specified equipment. Generally, the provider of any equipment retains legal ownership of (title to) the equipment.

Other forms of financing contracts, such as an installment sale agreement used typically for financing software licenses, exist and which generally contain terms and conditions similar to a conditional sale agreement, with variations to address different business aspects. To the extent that any of the alternative forms may be desirable, the reader should contact their financing counsel or determine what might be available from any potential third-party financing company.

The Basic Financing Forms

Equipment Leases

Leases fall into one of the two basic formats—the single transaction lease format and a master lease format. Although both follow the same fundamental structure, the lessor's format choice is dictated by the type of financing transaction, the relationship the lessor anticipates, and their document negotiation strategy. If the lessee has their own lease forms, the format choice is typically dictated by who has the greater negotiating leverage in a given relationship or transaction.

A checklist for drafting and negotiating a lease has been included in the Appendix.

The Single Transaction Lease

Lessors, particularly in small transaction third-party *vendor* programs (where the lessor has a committed relationship to provide financing for customers of an equipment seller) and in product vendor customer financing programs, frequently use a *standard* pre-printed single transaction lease. The standard single transaction lease form has fill-in blanks for those aspects, such as rent and equipment, that vary with each transaction. Although this type of lease format can be tailored to meet certain required variations, too many changes squeezed into the document margins, or attached as riders, can result in a document that is difficult to read. Traditionally, pre-printed single transaction leases have been used in small ticket (typically under 250,000 U.S. dollars in equipment cost) lease financings, but, today, an increasing number of lessors are using pre-printed lease forms for larger transactions, even as high as five million U.S. dollars, with negotiated changes addressed in an accompanying transaction drafted amendment.

The Master Lease

A lease format set up to permit future-needed equipment to be easily added is commonly referred to as a master lease. The master lease has two parts, a main, or *boilerplate*, portion containing the provisions that will remain the same from transaction to transaction (such as basic representations), and the second part, sometimes called a *schedule* containing the items that will vary among transactions (such as equipment type, rent, and purchase options). The advantage to using a master lease format is that the parties can document future transactions with a minimum amount of time and expense by merely adding a schedule containing essentially the business information relating to the specific transaction, such as equipment descriptions and payment terms.

Conditional Sale Agreement

The provisions of a conditional sale agreement are often similar to those found in a lease contract; the product user contractually agrees to pay for the equipment over a period of years and the *lender* gets assurance that the equipment will be kept in good condition in case it must be repossessed and sold to cover any payment default. In fact, a lease agreement with a one U.S. dollar, or bargain fixed priced, purchase option is considered a conditional sale agreement.

Managed Services Agreement

The reader is referred to Chapter 14 for an overview of a managed services agreements. This type of agreement states the terms and conditions under which the described services and, typically, equipment are provided and is generally subject to cancelation, as stated in the agreement terms, or implicitly for cause, such as for the failure to deliver services. This type of contract often requires some form of services provider financial support to be financeable by any lender or sold to a third-party financing company. There are no standard industry forms used.

Fee-Per-Use Agreement

The reader is referred to Chapter 14 for an overview of a fee-per-use agreement. This type of contract states the terms and conditions under which the described equipment, and, typically, related collateral deliverables, such as supplies, will be provided. It provides for periodic payments to be made based on the identified per-use conditions, such as a dollar amount for each time the equipment is used or the number of supplies that are used. It, as in the case of a services agreement, may also be subject to cancelation, as stated in the terms, or implicitly for cause, such as for the failure to deliver the stated deliverables to be used in connection with the equipment, and often requires some form of services provider financial support to be financeable by any lender or sold to a third-party financing company. There are no standard industry forms used.

Subjects to Address in a Lease

In putting together or reviewing lease forms and before starting and during any lease negotiations, the parties must understand the legal, financial, and practical aspects of a lease. To a large extent, these issues will also be present in a conditional sale agreement or an installment payment agreement and to a far less extent in a managed services or fee-per-use agreement.

The following explanation uses as a discussion base a net finance lease format because it is generally the most comprehensive and complex form. A net finance lease is a lease that is non-cancelable for its term and imposes all equipment ownership responsibilities, such as maintenance, on the equipment user, the lessee.

Party Identification

The lease for obvious reason should clearly state each party's full legal name, the jurisdiction in which each is organized, and the mailing address of their principal places of business.

Factual Summary

If the lease document is drafted specifically for a particular transaction, and not a pre-printed form, there should be a summary of the basic facts surrounding the transaction, such as describing any equipment purchase contract the lessee entered into prior to the lease, in what are referred to as *whereas clauses*, in the beginning part of the contract as a future reference for individuals not involved at the time the lease was negotiated.

Definitions of the Key Terms

The lease, particularly if it is a lengthy document, should, for ease of reference, define in one section the fundamental terms used repeatedly in the lease agreement, which have a special meaning, preferably at the document's beginning. For example, terms such as *fair market purchase value*, *purchase contract*, and *termination value* will usually have certain meanings in a particular transaction, and the parties must agree on their meaning to prevent future ambiguities.

Future-Delivered Equipment

Often, parties want to enter into a lease document well before the equipment's delivery date so that everyone knows the terms that have been agreed upon and, in the case of a lessee, to know their financing is in place at the time the equipment is delivered and must be paid for.

Putting Future-Delivered Equipment Under the Lease

When a lease transaction is documented before the equipment's delivery, the parties must prescribe a method for putting the equipment under lease when it arrives. Usually, the arrangement is for the lessee to notify the lessor in writing of the equipment's delivery and its acceptability for lease. The notification is typically contained in what is referred to as an *acceptance supplement*, or *delivery and acceptance certificate*, a written statement that lists the equipment delivered and states that the lessee has unconditionally accepted it for lease as of a specified date. If the equipment conforms to the lease agreement, it is automatically put on lease.

The Lease Term

The period of permitted use, the term of lease, is essential to state. Generally, there are two basic periods: (1) a main lease term, referred to as the *base lease term*, the *primary lease term*, or the *initial lease term* and (2) a renewal term. Some transactions, in addition, call for an *interim lease term*, also referred to as a *stub period*, beginning when the equipment becomes subject to lease until the start date of a predetermined base lease term. The interim term concept is frequently used when many equipment items will go on lease at various times. For example, the base term may start on January 1, 20XX, for all equipment delivered during the prior three-month period. By consolidating the start of the primary lease term to one date after which all equipment will be delivered, administrative work and rent payment mechanics are simplified.

The Rent Payment Structure

When the rent payments are due and how much they will be must be stated because they are key elements of every lease transaction. For example, a 10-year lease may call for rent to be payable in 20, consecutive, level, semi-annual in arrears payments, each payment to be equal to 1,000 U.S. dollars. The lease should also state what expenses, in addition to direct equipment cost, may be included, or *capitalized*, as part of the costs that will be financed, such as sales taxes, freight charges, and installation costs.

Payment Mechanism

To avoid rent receipt timing problems, the lease should specify: (1) where the rent is payable, such as at the lessor's place of business, (2) the form of payment, such as in immediately available U.S. funds, and (3) when it is to be deemed received by the lessor, such as when deposited in a U.S. mailbox or when the lessor has received immediately available funds.

Specifying the Rent Amount

Besides using fixed dollar amounts, the lease may express the rent due as a percentage of equipment cost. This is often done when equipment is to be delivered after the lease is signed, if there is the possibility that the cost may change. By using a rent percentage, the stated rent amount does not have to be recalculated if the purchase price varies from that anticipated. Additionally, when the rent is expressed as a percentage of equipment cost financed, any additional costs to be financed, such as sales taxes, freight charges, and installation costs, possibly unknown in amount when the lease is signed, can be easily determined when the amounts are known without requiring a lease amendment.

Tax Law Rental Adjustment

When a lessor's economic return depends in part on anticipated equipment ownership tax benefits, discussed in Chapter 11, they may want to make rent adjustments if unexpected tax law changes occur or a tax loss (recapture) occurs that adversely affects its economic return. For example, the lease may incorporate a provision that would allow the lessor to adjust the rent to maintain its *yield and after-tax cash flow* or maintain their *earnings* or *net return* if an adverse tax law change or tax loss occurs.

Conditions of Payment

In many equipment leases, particularly finance leases, the lessee's rent obligation is stated as absolute and unconditional. That is, the lessee must pay the rent in full and on time, regardless of any claim the lessee may have against the lessor or the equipment manufacturer. Commonly referred to as a *hell or high-water* obligation, the provision is not as troublesome as it seems initially because it does not prevent a lessee from independently bringing a lawsuit against the lessor or manufacturer on any claim.

Typically, a product vendor will want a hell or high-water provision included if it, for example, intends to borrow funds (by discounting the contract receivables) to finance the transaction using a nonrecourse loan to provide the lender with comfort that potential claims against the product vendor lessor would not affect the rental payment stream that is being relied on for the loan repayment.

Required Reports

A lessor will want to monitor the lease transaction by receiving certain reports from the lessee. At a minimum, the lessee will be required to provide annual financial reports if the lessee is not publicly held, accident reports, lease conformity reports, equipment location reports, and third-party claim reports.

Equipment Condition Provisions

Clearly, the equipment must always remain in good condition from a lessor's perspective, as it is both collateral for their investment and has the potential for additional profits when the lease ends.

Equipment Maintenance

A lease, as well as a conditional sale agreement, must specify which party has the obligation for equipment maintenance and what will be acceptable maintenance. Many types of leases, such as net finance leases, as well as conditional sale agreements, put the normal maintenance responsibilities on the lessee or obligor. Some managed services agreements often provide that the contract servicer will provide maintenance. Regardless of the arrangement, however, the maintenance issue should be specifically addressed.

Typically, in the case of a lease or conditional sale agreement, the agreement will specify the maintenance requirements in terms of the condition in which the equipment has to be maintained. A common provision requires the agreement obligor to keep the equipment in "good working order, ordinary wear and tear excepted." If the lessee, for example, could use the equipment in a manner that may cause extra wear and tear, the lessee may ask that the maintenance provision exclude ordinary wear and tear resulting from the lessee's intended use. And, if the equipment's manufacturer provides maintenance instructions, the agreement obligor should be required to follow them exactly.

Equipment Alterations

A lessee is typically prohibited from making equipment alterations not related to normal maintenance because an alteration could adversely affect the equipment's market value, thereby impairing its value to the lessor in a default repossession situation or following the end of the lease term.

Key Assurances Should be Required

Any contract providing equipment, including any that also provides services, should require that the contract equipment user or services recipient make certain key representations on matters related to the transaction, such as that the lessee or obligor is legally in existence and is authorized to enter into the contract, and should also provide that any failure to continue to comply with the representations would be an event of default, which would enable the lessor or obligee to declare an agreement breach and, thus, an agreement cancelation and, possibly, a claim for damages for breach.

Disclaimer of Product Responsibility

When the lessor is not the equipment vendor, the lessor will disclaim any responsibility for defects in the equipment's design, suitability, operation, fitness for use, and merchantability. If the lessor is the product vendor, doing so is not possible from a business standpoint, but may be acceptable if the disclaimer only applies to any contract assignee, such as a third-party transaction lender to the product vendor.

Risk of Loss

Generally, the lessee will bear the entire risk of equipment loss, whether due to damage, theft, requisition, or confiscation, because the lessee has possession of the equipment. Net finance leases often require the lessee to guarantee that the lessor will receive a minimum amount of money, usually referred to as the *stipulated loss value* or *casualty value*, if there is an equipment loss. This risk is typically covered by the lessee's property damage insurance, required to be obtained by the lessee and naming the lessor, as equipment owner, the sole loss payee.

General Tax Responsibility

In a typical net finance lease, the lessee is responsible for paying all taxes imposed by any local, state, or federal taxing authority other than on lessor's net income.

Tax Benefit Provisions

If the financing arrangement takes the form of a *true* lease for federal income tax purposes (see Chapter 11), lease provisions often ensure the desired tax treatment will not be compromised. If a lease does not qualify as a true tax lease, the lessor will undoubtedly lose ownership tax benefits, such as depreciation and any applicable investment tax credits, which would likely turn a profitable transaction into a highly unprofitable one. So, sophisticated tax-oriented lessors build in protections into the lease documentation in two basic ways—prohibiting inconsistent actions and filings that would cause a tax benefit loss and requiring tax indemnifications that make the lessor economically whole if there is a tax benefit loss, at a minimum, as the result of acts or omissions of the lessee.

Equipment Return Provisions

The condition in which and the place where the leased equipment must be returned to the lessor are important because of end-of-lease sale or re-leasing opportunities, something that a lessor may be relying on to maintain their anticipated economic return or something they are looking to for added profits. The best approach is to set an objective, easy-to-measure *outside* standard, for example, agreeing that an aircraft under lease will be returned with no less than 50 percent of remaining engine operation time before the next major overhaul. Where an easily measurable objective criterion is not available, the parties might agree to use an independent equipment appraiser to assess the equipment's condition.

The lease should also specify where the equipment is to be returned and who will bear the delivery expense. If, at the lease's end, a lessor, for example, unexpectedly had to pay for the transportation of 200 trucks from 10 of a lessee's plants scattered up and down the East Coast to a central sale point in the Midwest, their profit margin could be adversely affected. Although who pays for shipping expenses varies with each transaction, it is not unusual for one point of delivery that is relatively near the lessee's location of use to be agreed upon.

Events of Default

If a problem arises that would jeopardize the lessor's rights or interest in the lease or the equipment, as with any other financing contract, the lessor should be in a position to end the contract and take any other action that may be appropriate, such as reclaiming the equipment. The various *problem* situations that could give rise to this type of lease right should be clearly specified in every lease agreement and are generally referred to as *events of default*. These *events* include, for example, the non-payment of any rent or other payment obligations, the failure to comply with any non-payment obligations, or an unauthorized equipment transfer.

Lessor's Remedies Following an Event of Default

In addition to what will be stated events of default, the lease contract should set out what remedies the lessor can pursue if a lessee defaults, such as immediate termination of the contract and the repossession of the equipment and specific monetary damages. The various remedies listed in a lease sometimes overlap, but from a lessor's viewpoint, it is better to be somewhat redundant than to risk a claim that a certain course of action was waived by implication because it was omitted. Additionally, many of the rights stated exist in law whether they are specifically stated.

Court Action

The most obvious default remedy that is frequently stated is a right to bring a court action to require the lessee to perform any breached obligation or to get money damages for the failure to do so. Even if not so stated, this is one that is always available under contract law.

Termination of the Lease

The lessor's right to terminate a lessee's rights under the lease, including their right to use the equipment, is a basic default remedy. As a part of this right, a lease usually states that the lessor can enter the lessee's premises immediately and take possession of the equipment. The reclaiming right is particularly useful when a lessee's creditors are trying to attach assets as security for their claims, but it has some limitations if the lessee is in bankruptcy, as discussed in Chapter 15.

Redelivery of the Equipment

Lessors commonly have the right to require a lessee to redeliver the equipment in an event of default section, once again, subject to some limitations if the lessee is in bankruptcy. This redelivery obligation usually imposes a greater burden than if the lease normally ran its course. For example, the lessee may have to redeliver the equipment at their own expense and risk to any location that the lessor designates, rather than to the nearest general transportation pickup point. In an adversary proceeding, the expanded right may not have much more meaning than helping to measure damages because a great deal of cooperation cannot be expected from the lessee.

Storage of the Equipment

In a default situation, the lessor may not have a place to readily store the equipment. Thus, the lessor may want to obligate the lessee to store the equipment on their premises, free of charge, until the lessor can dispose of it following a default. Whether or not it is advisable to let a lessee in financial trouble retain control over the equipment is a separate issue that would have to be considered by the lessor when a default occurs. For example, a lessor may run the risk that other creditors would seize the equipment even though the creditors do not have a valid claim, with possible re-renting time lost and potential equipment deterioration that could endanger the lessor's equipment residual (end of lease) investment or profit opportunity.

Sale of the Equipment

A lessor will often include a lease provision that provides, after a lessee defaults, that they can sell or otherwise dispose of the leased equipment, free and clear of any of the lessee's rights, again subject to some limitations if the lessee is in bankruptcy. However, savvy lessees typically request the right to have an offset of any proceeds received against any damages they may owe.

Right to Hold or Re-Lease the Equipment

Besides being able to dispose of the equipment, a lessor would want the right to "hold, use, operate, lease to others, or keep idle" any equipment that they have re-acquired as a result of a lease default. Ideally, then, a lessor can take whatever action they deem to be in the best interest. Of course, if a court finds that the lessor did not act in a manner to minimize the damages suffered, it may limit any recovery that a lessor may be able to get.

Liquidated Damages

A *liquidated damage* provision should always be included as an alternative default remedy. Under this type of provision, the parties agree on a method for determining what damages the lessor is entitled to if a default occurs. Generally, courts will uphold a liquidated damage arrangement if it fairly anticipates the losses that may result from the lessee's non-performance and is not deemed to be a penalty.

Although there is often no actual definitive way to measure the actual damages that a lessor would suffer because of a lessee's default, there are two formulas that are frequently used. One provides for the lessee to pay an amount equal to the present value of the aggregate remaining rentals that the lessor would have received, but for the default, reduced by the equipment's fair market sales value or the present worth of the equipment's fair market rental value over the original remaining lease term. The other calls for the payment of an amount equal to the equipment's stipulated loss value (which is typically the lessor's remaining investment principal and interest as of the date of default, possibly reduced by the equipment's fair market sales value or the present worth of the equipment's fair market rental value over the original remaining lease term). A prescribed per annum discount rate, such as the prime commercial lending rate in effect at the time of termination, is often incorporated into the liquidated damage *formula* for present worth computation purposes.

A Lessor Needs Certain Lease Assignment Rights

Lessors insert in a lease the right to assign their lease interest and the equipment at any time during the term, without notice to or consent from the lessee. While a general assignment right sometimes makes prospective lessees uneasy, it generally does not cause a concern if the assignment provision also provides that none of the lessor's duties or obligations will be assigned or that the assignment will not adversely affect the lessee's lease rights. This type of right is particularly important when a lessor wants the ability to borrow a portion of the equipment purchase cost from a lender on a recourse or nonrecourse basis by discounting the contract receivables. And, to do that, the lessor usually must assign to the lender all the lessor's lease contract rights, such as the right to receive uninterrupted rentals. Additionally, a lessor may also want the ability to *sell* the lease, including the title to the equipment, to a third party. In this case, the third-party buyer would become the equipment owner, would be required to take subject to the terms and conditions of the lease agreement, and would, therefore, become the *lessor*. The original lessor would no longer have any rights or possibly duties under the lease.

A Lessee May Want Certain Equipment Sublease Rights

A lessee with the right to sublease equipment is in the best position to lessen or eliminate the impact of having to pay rent on assets that have become unproductive because of changes in use needs during the lease term. If there are no restrictions, such as those that would limit transfers to affiliated companies only, a lessee will have the maximum flexibility.

Lessor's Options to Renew, Sell, or Terminate

There are a very few situations when a lessor will want certain rights, ones that are not usually requested, such as a right to terminate the lease in a non-default situation, a right to force a sale of the equipment to the lessee, a right to force the lessee to renew a lease, or a right to abandon the equipment. These rights, however, can create substantial true lease tax problems or be otherwise undesirable from a lessee's viewpoint and should be used with caution.

The Right to Terminate the Lease

It is conceivable, although extremely unlikely, that a lessor would want to be able to terminate a lease for any reason they choose during its term without the lessee's consent. For example, if a lessor believes the rental market will rise before the end of the negotiated lease term, they may want to have the ability to get the equipment back and lease it at a higher rental rate.

The Right to Force a Sale of the Equipment to the Lessee

In certain situations, a lessor will insist on having the right (commonly referred to as a *put*) to force a lessee to buy the equipment under lease at the end of the term. Generally, this right is expressed as a fixed percentage of the original equipment's cost rather than a defined dollar amount. For example, a lessor may have the right to sell the equipment to the lessee for an amount equal to 10 percent of the cost. In effect, a put eliminates any risk that a lessor will not realize its assumed residual value that, in turn, protects its anticipated profit. Transactions involving certain types of store fixtures or equipment that will be difficult or uneconomical to move, such as certain heavy storage tanks, sometimes incorporate a forced sale right. This right, in particular, will have adverse tax consequences, causing the lease to no longer qualify as a true lease for tax purposes.

The Right to Abandon the Equipment

In the past, equipment abandonment rights had been used in leases of equipment that would be difficult and costly, if not totally impractical, to reclaim if the lessee decided not to buy it at the end of the term. A good example of the type of leases that involved abandonment rights were those relating to certain kinds of commercial storage tanks that were so large that the only way to move them was to cut them into pieces and then re-weld them at the new site. In these situations, the expenses involved could be so great that the lessor could not reasonably recoup them through a releasing or a sale.

Lessors sometimes attempt to solve an equipment removal expense problem by requiring the equipment to be delivered to them at the end of the term at the lessee's expense. If the lessee refuses to do so, however, the lessor's only recourse, without a right of abandonment, would be to bring a lawsuit to force the lessee to live up to their agreement or, possibly, pay for any resulting damages. If the lessee is in financial trouble, a lawsuit may be of little use. Having an abandonment right allows the lessor to drop the property in the lessee's lap and rid themselves of any lingering responsibility or expense exposure.

The Right to Require a Lease Renewal

In situations where an abandonment right or a put might be considered, a lessor may instead use a forced lease renewal right. Under this right, a lessor could make the lessee re-lease the equipment at a predetermined rental. This right may have adverse tax consequences, causing the lease to no longer qualify as a true lease for tax purposes.

Lessee Options to Buy, Renew, Terminate, or Upgrade the Equipment

Invariably, a prospective lessee will ask for certain rights, referred to as *options*, that will enable them to maintain some form of control over the equipment's use or operating condition, such as an equipment purchase right, a lease renewal right, a lease termination right, or an equipment upgrade right. Generally, these types of options are willingly granted by lessors. Typically, these rights will not cause adverse tax consequences, causing the lease to fail as a true lease (discussed in Chapter 12) for income tax purposes.

The Right to Buy the Equipment at Fair Market Value

A prospective lessee may want to be able to buy the leased equipment at the lease's end. In many situations, this is done through a fair market value purchase option. Basically, the option gives the lessee the right to buy the equipment for whatever its fair market value is at the time it is exercised.

Although the term *fair market value* may appear self-explanatory, the parties should agree on a method for its determination. Generally, the *fair market value* of an item of equipment is the amount that a willing buyer under no compulsion to purchase would pay a willing seller under no compulsion to sell in the open market. As a practical matter, however, how is the value determined between a lessor and a lessee? Typically, it is done by an agreement between the parties, and if they cannot agree, then through an equipment appraisal. If appraisal must be used, the parties can designate in the lease an independent appraiser who will evaluate the equipment at the appropriate time. Alternatively, the parties can each select an independent appraiser to make an assessment when necessary. If the two appraisers cannot agree on a satisfactory value, then they often must jointly select a third appraiser, whose opinion will be binding.

The Right to Buy the Equipment at a Fixed Price

In the case of equipment that has traditionally maintained a favorable re-sale value, many companies refuse to lease because a fair market purchase option coupled with the lease rents could result in an economically unfavorable way of acquiring it. As a result, a fixed price purchase option is sometimes given to induce them to lease. Under the fixed price purchase option, commonly referred to as a *call*, the lessee can buy the equipment at the end of the lease for a predetermined price. The price is usually expressed as a percentage of the equipment's original cost. For example, the lessee may have the right to buy designated equipment for 35 percent of the cost. In this way, the lessee knows the maximum amount of money they will have to spend if they want to buy the equipment when the lease is over. This right, if the option purchase price is considered a bargain, will result in adverse true lease tax consequences.

The Right to Renew the Lease at Fair Rental Value

Providing a lessee with the right to renew a lease at the equipment's fair market rental value at the time of renewal is acceptable, both from the standpoint of the Internal Revenue Service and, generally, a lessor. The parties can determine the fair market rental amount in a manner like that of the determination of the fair market purchase value, through independent appraisal at the time of the intended renewal.

The Right to Renew the Lease at a Fixed Price

Prospective lessees sometimes request a fixed price renewal option. By knowing in advance the exact dollar amount of the renewal rents, they know where they would economically stand if they wanted to continue to use the equipment beyond the main lease term. This would, of course, not be possible with the fair market renewal option. This right may also result in adverse true lease tax consequences.

The Right to Terminate the Lease

It is not uncommon for a lessee to want the ability to terminate a lease early, particularly when they believe the equipment could become technically obsolete or surplus to their needs before the lease would normally end. When this right is granted, the lessee frequently will be required to pay the lessor a predetermined amount of money, commonly referred to as the *termination value*, on exercise. Because most lessors do not like to grant termination rights, the termination amount is usually high and will repay the lessor any remaining investment balance due with interest at least to the date of termination, plus a profit.

The Right of First Refusal

A lessee purchase *right of first refusal* is sometimes used as an alternative to a fair market value purchase option. Under this option, a lessee is given the right to buy the leased equipment at the end of the lease term under the same terms and conditions as offered by an unaffiliated third party. The disadvantage to using it is that a lessee may run the risk that a competitor may bid for the equipment either to push the price up or to acquire it for their own operations.

The Right to Upgrade Financing

At times, companies lease equipment, such as computer systems, that may require upgrading during the lease term to ensure maximum performance, such as adding additional equipment or modifying the original equipment. Typically, an upgrade may not be done without the lessor's prior written consent and, in some situations, it may be of such a nature, for example, that requires internal equipment modifications that have no standalone value and, as a result, no one other than the original lessor would consider financing it. In these situations, the incumbent lessor has absolute negotiating control over the financing and can charge the lessee more than the going market rate.

A Defaulting Party Should Lose Certain Options

Generally, a lease will provide that the party holding an option will forfeit any option to exercise rights if it is in default under the lease. For example, lessee should lose their right to buy the equipment under a purchase option because of default on their part.

Designate the Law Governing the Lease

It is always advisable for the parties to specify what jurisdiction's law will apply to their rights and obligations under a lease agreement. For example, the parties can agree that all actions on lease issues will be decided under the laws of the state of New York, regardless of whether the proceedings are instituted in a New York court. By doing this, the attorneys can draft the documents under the law they believe will give the fairest known outcome.

Severability Clause

A lease will typically include a severability clause, providing that any lease provision determined to be legally unenforceable will be severed. In other words, the severed provision will be treated as though it never existed to prevent the entire lease agreement from being held invalid if only certain provisions are unenforceable.

The Interest Penalty for Late Payments

A lease agreement will generally prescribe an interest rate that will be charged on any overdue payments, such as delinquent rent payments. This eliminates disputes over late charge penalties and assists in assessing damages if a lawsuit arises.

The Lease Should Identify Where and How to Send any Required Notifications

While leases usually provide that all required notifications and payments, such as loss notifications, must be promptly made, they sometimes fail to identify exactly where they should be sent. As a result, notifications could be misdirected and valuable time lost. In addition to specifying the address where and notifications must be sent, the lease should also specify the notification manner. For example, it may be agreed that a notice will be deemed, given when it is deposited in a U.S. mailbox, sent by prepaid certified mail.

The Lease Should be Correctly Signed

All parties to a lease should make sure it is signed in the proper capacities. Leases to be signed by an individual representing himself or herself generally do not present any problems. Leases to be signed by an individual representing a business entity, such as a limited partnership, corporation, or trust, sometimes do. If, in the latter case, the signature is not made in the correct representative capacity, the represented firm may not be bound, but the individual signer may be personally liable. For example, if a vice president intends to sign on behalf of his or her corporation, the signature block should have the company name as well as the individual's name and title. If the signature is not correct, for example, if the signing individual's title is missing, he or she may run the risk that he or she is personally liable on the contract and the business entity is not bound to the contract; certainly, a less-than-desirable outcome for all parties concerned.

Subjects to Address in Drafting and Negotiating a Conditional Sale Agreement

The Similarities to a Lease

The provisions that should be included in a conditional sale agreement are similar to those that should be included in a lease contract. For example, the default provisions are typically similar, such as repossession of equipment and liquidated damages in the amount of the remaining payments.

The Key Difference

Because in a conditional sale agreement, the user of the equipment is deemed to be the owner of the equipment, whether equipment title is transferred to the equipment user at the start or at the end of the conditional sale contract, tax indemnification provisions for loss of tax benefits typically found in leases are omitted as unnecessary.

Subjects to Address in Drafting and Negotiating Managed Services and Fee-Per-Use Agreements

There are no typical forms used for managed services and fee-per-use agreements, as there are for equipment leases and conditional sale agreements, so each contract must be reviewed for business and legal aspects. Clearly, the services and fee-per-use pricing, discussed in Chapter 14, are important for both the services provider and the end user. For the service providers providing equipment in these contracts, they will attempt to ensure that the contract pricing will, at a minimum, amortize the cost of the equipment (less any equipment residual value assumed at the end of the contract term), along with their profit, in the contract payment pricing. This may involve providing for a minimum charge that occurs monthly or, at least, over the term of the contract, unless the services provider is willing to use as their business model a form of month-to-month or period-to-period rental arrangement, anticipating that the equipment can be readily re-used for other transactions, something not typically entertained by a services provider without a strong end user secondary market. Generally, the contract default arrangements involve a repossession of the equipment and, possibly, some form of liquidated damages provision that recoups the payments that would otherwise be due. However, as these agreements typically contain a provision that allows the obligor to terminate the agreement for convenience, defaults are generally not a major issue.

Summary

The lease or other financing document sets out the business arrangement to which both the financing party, such as the lessor, and the obligor, such as the lessee, have agreed. They, of course, must be carefully reviewed and written, covering all aspects that may or should come into play in the financing arrangement. This cannot be done without understanding each aspect of a typical lease or other financing contract.

CHAPTER 10

Closing the Financing Contract

Overview

Once the terms and conditions of a financing contract are agreed on, certain additional documents, referred to as *collateral* documents, may be required to *close* a financing transaction. These collateral, or supplemental, documents range from the ones that essentially provide comfort on specified issues, such as opinions of counsel, to the ones that address critical support arrangements, such as a contract guaranty.

Although drafting the supplemental papers will be the responsibility of the transaction's lawyers, the business people should understand the fundamental concepts involved so that any forms can be meaningfully reviewed to ensure they accurately reflect the agreements reached. Also, understanding the purpose of the collateral documents will enable the business participants to comfortably negotiate compromises when the lawyers reach impasses. And, that is the purpose of this chapter—to provide you with a closing document overview so that you know in advance what to expect and enable you to facilitate smooth transaction closings.

One final point before we begin. While this chapter provides a general working knowledge of the typical collateral lease documents, keep in mind that many transactions may have their own unique aspects that must also be considered.

A supplemental lease document closing checklist has been included in the Appendix.

Legal Opinions

The Function of Legal Opinions

In large ticket (multi-million dollar) and, at times, middle market (under one million U.S. dollars) financing transactions, legal opinions are typically required by the financing party and, in some cases, by sophisticated lessees. A legal opinion does not guarantee that the conclusions expressed in the opinion are correct. A court or administrative agency may interpret the law based on the facts or otherwise differently than expressed in an opinion—and their decision, not the legal opinion, will be controlling. It does, however, provide the participants with a significant degree of comfort as expressed because the lawyer's opinion will typically have been well researched.

Unfortunately, legal opinions are invariably qualified by, for example, stating a very specific set of facts on which they are based. To the extent that the relevant facts are not properly conveyed to the lawyer providing the opinion, therefore, the opinion may be of little or no value. Additionally, in drafting a legal opinion, the lawyer will need access to relevant information and, therefore, writing it may bring to light transaction trouble spots that need to be corrected if possible. And, finally, the *expertness* of the lawyer providing an opinion is a critical consideration, particularly when complex legal or tax issues are involved. Therefore, if you need a legal opinion in a lease or other financing transaction, choose a lawyer with solid, relevant experience.

Opinion from Lessee's or Obligor's Counsel

The goal of the lessee's, or contact obligor's, counsel's opinion is to provide the financing party with assurances that no legal issues exist that will undermine the financing transaction, including that:

- the lessee or contract obligor has been properly organized, is validly in existence, and is in good standing under the laws of their state of organization;
- the lessee or contract obligor has the authority to enter into the financing agreement;

- the lessee or contract obligor can perform all their lease or financing agreement obligations;
- all of the lessee's or contract obligor's financing agreement commitments are legally binding;
- any consents, such as those of shareholders, that are necessary have been obtained;
- any regulatory approvals, such as a state public utility commission, that are necessary, as well as all other proper action, have been taken;
- there are no adverse pending or threatened court or administrative proceedings against the lessee or contract obligor and, if there are, their probable outcome; and
- the lessee or contract obligor will not violate any law, rule, or provision of any of their existing agreements by entering into the lease or financing arrangement or complying with any of its terms.

Opinions from Lessor's Counsel

In certain lease situations, particularly multi-million dollar transactions, where there will be future-delivered equipment (equipment delivered after the lease is signed), a lessee, or their counsel, might ask for an opinion from the lessor's counsel concerning the lessor's legal ability to enter into and perform their obligations, including, that it is

- properly incorporated or organized, as the case may be, at the time the lease is signed, and
- qualified to do business in the jurisdiction where the equipment will be used to avoid, for example, any risk that the equipment could be attached by the jurisdictional authorities for the nonpayment of any taxes that the lessor may owe.

Opinion from the Guarantor's Counsel

In the case of a weak credit, a guarantor of the lessee's or obligor's contract obligations may be desirable. In this case, the strength and viability of the guarantor's commitment is critical, and to support the financing contract, a favorable opinion from the guarantor's counsel may be required, covering issues such as that:

- the guarantor is duly organized, validly existing, and in good standing;
- nothing exists that could adversely affect the guarantee's quality, such as material litigation;
- the guarantee has been fully and properly authorized; and
- the guarantee is a legally enforceable obligation.

Opinion from the Product Seller's Counsel

Typically, the equipment vendor is not asked to provide any legal opinion because they only must deliver clear title to the equipment, and an adequate bill of sale containing proper seller representations and warranties generally provides the necessary comfort. In certain situations, particularly in large multi-million-dollar transactions, the equipment vendor may be asked to provide a legal opinion confirming that the vendor has, upon equipment payment, delivered clear title to the equipment.

Financial Information

For a product vendor with an in-house financing activity, particularly if the product vendor wants to discount the receivables or sell the financing contract to a bank or third-party leasing company, they should consider the need for obtaining from any privately held customer, and any privately held guarantor, updates to any financial information previously provided, certainly for transactions in excess, generally, of 250,000 U.S. dollars. This, of course, should be coordinated when possible with any third-party financing contract lender or purchaser because their financial information requirements may be different. For customers who are publicly held, financial information is readily available, but updates may not be.

Business Authorization Documents

A product vendor financing a customer should consider, in cases of transactions generally in excess of 250,000 U.S. dollars, requiring a copy of the customer's board of directors' resolutions or other documentation, as applicable, authorizing the transaction. A typical lessee corporate resolution, for example, will state that the lessee has been duly authorized to enter into the transaction for the specified dollar amount, and that a certain person has been authorized to execute the documents on behalf of the corporation.

Guarantees and Other Financial Support

If a product vendor customer wants to lease or finance more equipment than their credit capability justifies, they will be asked for additional credit support, such as a guaranty from a financially strong third party or parent company or through a letter of credit.

The most favorable guaranty is a full customer contract guaranty, where the guarantor unconditionally obligates himself or herself to ensure the obligor's full and prompt performance of all the financing contract obligations, covenants, and conditions. For example, if a lessee fails to pay the rent, the lessor could go directly to the guarantor for payment. A partial guaranty may also be acceptable, where the guarantor, for example, is only responsible for the partial repayment of the total contract lease or financing payments.

Proof of Insurance Documents

Typically, a financing contract will require that the obligor have third-party personal injury and property damage insurance covering the financed equipment, particularly if it is leased or otherwise owned by the financing party. The insurance should be in place when the equipment is accepted by the customer for financing, confirmed by the delivery of a certificate of insurance from the customer's insurance company. Additionally, the insurance certificate should state that the required insurance coverage may not be canceled without prior written notice to the financing party, and then only, after an adequate grace period, to give the financing party an opportunity to obtain insurance if the contract obligor fails to keep it in force.

Equipment Purchase Agreements

It is always advisable for a lessor to have the product user enter into a purchase agreement directly with the product vendor. However, if the product vendor is providing the financing, they should have a financing proposal in place, signed by the customer, that states the terms of the expected financing arrangement, including the equipment to be acquired and which contains, or is supplemented by, a customer product purchase order. A purchase order is advisable as a fallback equipment obligation in case the customer decides not to lease the equipment. If the financing arrangement includes third-party equipment, then a separate purchase order or agreement between the third-party supplier and the financed customer is advisable, and an assignment of the right, but not the obligation, to buy be given to the financing company. In this case, a warranty bill of sale, discussed below, should also be provided to the financing company covering the third-party equipment.

An Equipment Bill of Sale

In a typical lease situation, the product vendor provides a lessor with a warranty bill of sale (which transfers equipment title free and clear of all liens, claims, and encumbrances) when it pays for the equipment. When the product vendor is also the lessor, this is not necessary, other than to document the equipment transaction between any in-house financing company if a separate entity, and the product vendor. If the product vendor has a financing affiliate, this could be done using, in effect, a *blanket* bill of sale that applies to all inter-company financing transfers. However, as stated earlier, if there is third-party equipment included as part of the financing, then a third-party equipment supplier warranty bill of sale is advisable for the equipment.

Waivers from Landowners or Mortgagees

If the financed equipment is located on real property the lessee or obligor leases from a third party or is subject to a mortgage, the financing party should obtain from the landlord or mortgagee an agreement that it will not prevent the repossession of any leased or secured equipment in the case of contract default. Accordingly, to avoid issues, a financing party should require a waiver from the landlord or mortgagee of any claim to the financed equipment.

Security Interest Filings

Although not technically necessary in a typical equipment lease situation, a product vendor acting as a lessor should generally file appropriate, information-only Uniform Commercial Code (UCC) financing statements, discussed in Chapter 13, to provide added assurance that it, in fact, has priority over other parties who may claim an interest in the equipment, particularly the customer's creditors. A UCC financing statement filing is necessary if the lease is, in fact, a conditional sale or the financing contract is in effect a loan transaction to secure a financing party's collateral rights in the equipment over other creditors of the transaction customer. Simple in form, a UCC financing statement basically requires nothing more than a description of the parties, with their addresses, and the equipment. The UCC financing statement filing should generally be a condition of the lease or other financing contract closing and should be made in the state of organization of the obligor. The filing procedures are routine, and the expenses are nominal and can be accomplished by one of many companies providing UCC filing services, such as Cogency Global (www.cogencyglobal.com/ucc-filing-services).

Managed Services and Fee-Per-Use Agreement Supplemental Documents

Typically, there are little to no collateral documents required in the case of managed services and fee-per-use agreements; however, if the receivables are to be assigned to a third-party lender, these agreements are often accompanied by a few basic additional documents, such as a basic opinion of counsel, typically the obligor's in-house counsel, and a letter from the obligor's in-house counsel affirming the due authorization and execution of the contract. In any event, if you, as a product vendor, have a potential third-party financing company that you intend to sell the contract and equipment to, or discount the contract receivable with, you should coordinate any collateral document needs with the financing company at the start of the customer financing discussion.

Summary

The supplemental documents that accompany the closing of a lease or other financing transaction must not be overlooked until the last minute. These documents can give rise to problems or concerns or issues that can prevent or unduly delay a lease or other type financing transaction closing. Understanding what they are, and how they work, will facilitate avoiding costly closing issues.

CHAPTER 11

Tax Aspects of Financing Transactions

Introduction

A lessor's ability to write off, depreciate, the cost of the leased equipment can be a key income component in an equipment lease transaction. Prior to 1986, another important equipment ownership tax benefit was available, a 10 percent equipment investment tax credit (ITC), eliminated completely by the 1986 Tax Reform Act (TRA), except for certain transition property. In recent years, an ITC up to 30 percent became available for limited types of equipment, such as wind and solar equipment, as well as fuel cells, often referred to as energy tax credits, which will, at the time of this writing, generally begin to wind down starting in 2020. Like other tax credits, the ITC does not merely reduce taxable income, but rather offsets, dollar-for-dollar, the equipment owner's federal income tax liability.

How to determine the amount of equipment ownership tax benefits available for a product vendor for assets transferred to and financed through its financing activity is a determination that should be made with its tax accountants based on how the activity is set up. In the case of a conditional sale agreement or other equipment financing contract, the aforementioned equipment ownership tax benefits are available only to the obligor of the financing transaction, who, in fact, is, for tax purposes, the equipment owner.

Investment Tax Credit: An Overview

As an equipment tax credit, at the time of this writing, is not a generally available tax benefit except as stated earlier, a detailed discussion of how tax credits work is beyond the scope of this book. However, in the government's on-again, off-again pursuit of economic stimulus, as it is still possible that some form of general equipment tax credit, beyond the current available energy tax credits, will again reappear, a brief explanation is of use.

Basically, the purpose of tax credits is to encourage investment in new equipment to stimulate economic growth. The tax writers also used them to encourage the growth, development, and stabilization of a business area that the federal government seeks to promote, such as in the energy area.

An ITC permits an equipment owner to offset its federal income tax liability by an amount equal to a specified percentage of the cost (technically, *basis*) of equipment acquired and placed in service in a tax year. Thus, for example, a taxpayer, including an equipment lessor, buying energy equipment in 2019 that cost one million U.S. dollars for which a 30 percent ITC is available could reduce its federal income tax liability by an amount equal to 300,000 U.S. dollars (30% × $1 million = $300,000) for 2019. It should be kept in mind that the lessor is only entitled to claim energy-related tax credits, and available depreciation, for equipment under lease if the lease qualifies as a *true* lease for federal income tax purposes, discussed in Chapter 12.

Equipment Depreciation: An Overview

Assets owned, for example, by a leasing and financing company can be depreciated under rules stated in the Modified Accelerated Cost Recovery System (MACRS) in Section 168 of the 1986 TRA. Basically, depreciation allows the equipment owner to recoup its equipment investment over time, the depreciation period, and is an income tax deduction that the equipment owner can use to offset, as an expense, their gross taxable income.

Under MACRS, there are three depreciation methods, six recovery periods, and two averaging conventions that apply to equipment, depending on a variety of factors.

Property Eligible for MACRS

Besides meeting the MACRS requirements, to be depreciable, equipment must qualify under Internal Revenue Code (*IRC*) Section 167(a).

Section 167 establishes the basic rule authorizing an equipment owner to a deduction, in computing federal income tax liability, for the exhaustion, wear, and tear of property used in a trade or business or held for the production of income. All depreciation deductions under MACRS must fulfill the stated threshold requirements, that is, the property must be depreciable (subject to wearing out) and must be used in a business or income producing activity.

Generally, property qualifying under Section 167(a) may be depreciated under MACRS. Intangible property, property classified as public utility property (unless the taxpayer uses a normalization method of accounting), certain property that a lessor has elected to apply a depreciation method not expressed in terms of years (such as the unit of production method), motion picture films, video tapes, sound recordings (such as music tapes), and property covered by MACRS anti-churning or transition rules are not eligible for MACRS depreciation. Additionally, certain other property must be depreciated under an alternative MACRS method, described later in this chapter.

How are the MACRS Deductions Computed?

Four steps determine the annual MACRS depreciation deduction amount for any equipment. First, the total amount (*basis*) to be depreciated is determined; next, the applicable MACRS recovery class is selected; third, the appropriate depreciation method is applied; and, fourth, the applicable convention is incorporated.

Total Amount to be Depreciated

The total amount an equipment owner can write off, and thus the annual deduction amount, depends on the owner's basis in the equipment. For MACRS purposes, basis is determined under general IRC rules for determining the gain or loss on the sale or other disposition of an asset and includes not only what the equipment owner paid for the equipment, but also the costs incurred in acquiring the equipment. However, an equipment owner must reduce the basis so calculated by any amount expensed under Section 179, discussed in Section F, by any amount claimed as a first-year bonus depreciation and, if a tax credit is available and claimed, such as an energy tax credit, to account for that credit. There is, however, no reduction for equipment salvage value.

In the case of a product vendor with an in-house financing operation, the basis for products financed will need to be assessed by their tax accountants.

MACRS Recovery Classes

The MACRS recovery class determines the period over which depreciation deductions can be taken. So, the equipment owner must determine if the equipment falls within the IRS stated 3-Year Property Class, 5-Year Property Class, 7-Year Property Class, 10-Year Property Class, 15-Year Property Class, or 20-Year Property Class. For example, cars, light and heavy general-purpose trucks, computer and peripheral equipment, trailers, and trailer-mounted containers are examples of types of equipment that come within the five-year property class.

Depreciation Methods

Under MACRS, an equipment owner recovers the equipment's cost over the number of years in the recovery class plus one; for example, three-year property yields deductions over a four-year period. For equipment in the 3-, 5-, 7-, or 10-year class, a lessor generally uses the 200 percent declining balance method of depreciation, discussed next, with a switch to straight-line depreciation at the time that maximizes the deduction, taking into account the half-year or mid-quarter convention, also discussed next. For property in the 15- and 20-year classes, a lessor generally uses the 150 percent declining balance method with a switch to the straight-line method at a time that maximizes the deduction, considering the half-year or mid-quarter convention. Instead of the applicable declining balance method, a straight-line or alternative method of depreciation may be elected, discussed next.

Under the declining balance method, the equipment owner calculates the depreciation deduction for any year by multiplying the asset's basis-reduced by any prior years' depreciation deductions—by the declining balance rate, and then multiplying by the percent available each year. Thus, for example, for an asset with a 100 U.S. dollar basis and a five-year recovery period, using the 200 percent declining balance method, the first year's depreciation is 40 U.S. dollars (ignoring the averaging conventions):

$$\$100 \text{ basis} \times 2 \times 20\% = \$40$$

For the second year, the MACRS deduction would be 24 U.S. dollars:

$$\$100 \text{ basis} - \$40 \text{ first-year deduction} = \$60$$
$$\$60 \times 2 \times 20\% = \$24$$

And so on, for three more years.

At the point when the declining balance method yields smaller deductions than straight line, the method switches to straight line. The 200 percent balance method resulted in more accelerated deductions than had been available under the previously available depreciation guidelines (the Accelerated Cost Recover System, or ACRS). The Internal Revenue Service (IRS) has calculated and published, in Revenue Procedure 87–57 (IRB 1987-42), the appropriate annual deductions applying the 200 percent and 150 percent methods for each MACRS recovery class.

As stated earlier, a lessor can elect to use the straight-line depreciation method instead of the prescribed MACRS accelerated method established for MACRS property classes. Once an election is made, it is irrevocable (unless consented to by the IRS) and applies to all the MACRS eligible property within the same asset class that is placed in service during the relevant tax year. The assets within the class for which a straight-line method is elected are to be written-off over the recovery period prescribed under the applicable regular recovery period.

MACRS Averaging Conventions

In calculating depreciation deductions, the handling of placements in, and retirements from, service that occur during the year must be addressed. Generally, under MACRS, a lessor recovers equipment costs using the half-year convention. Under that convention, equipment is deemed to have been placed in service at the mid-point of the year in which it was placed in service, regardless of when during the year it was placed in service. Similarly, an asset is deemed to have been disposed of, or retired from service, at the mid-point of the year during which it was disposed of or retired, regardless of when, in fact, it was disposed of or retired during the year. Thus, a lessor is entitled to one-half a full year's permitted depreciation in the year it places an eligible asset in service, and one-half a full year's depreciation in the year it disposes of or retires the asset from service. However, if more that 40 percent of the aggregate basis (essentially, cost) of property placed in during a taxable year is placed in service during the last three months of that year, the mid-quarter convention applies. Under this convention, the first-year depreciation for all MACRS property (with a few exceptions, such as for nonresidential real property) placed in service during the tax year is computed based on the number of quarters that the property was in service, with property placed in service anytime during a quarter being treated as having been placed in service at the mid-point of the quarter.

The Alternative MACRS Depreciation Method

An alternative depreciation system (ADS) must be used in certain select cases, but can be elected in other situations. Under ADS, a taxpayer generally computes their permitted depreciation allowance by applying the straight-line method, without making a basis reduction for salvage value, over a recovery period typically longer than that specified under the other MACRS approaches. The applicable averaging conventions—the half-year or mid-quarter convention—apply in the same situations as under the regular MACRS.

When must ADS be Used?

A taxpayer must use ADS to depreciate equipment used predominantly outside the United States, that is, when it is located for more than 50 percent of the time during a tax year outside the United States. ADS must also be used for tax-exempt bond financed property, basically property financed out of the proceeds of tax-exempt bonds, tax-exempt use property, such as equipment leased to a tax-exempt entity, and equipment generally produced or manufactured in a foreign country.

When can ADS be Elected?

A taxpayer can elect to use ADS for any MACRS property for any MACRS eligible tax year, but the election is irrevocable and applies to all property in the class that the taxpayer has placed in service during the election year.

ADS Recovery Periods

Under ADS, a taxpayer will generally depreciate the equipment over the ADR class life period as stated in Revenue Procedure 87–56. The class life period is five years, for example, for automobiles, light general-purpose trucks, and qualified technological equipment.

Depreciation Recapture

Generally, on the disposition of MACRS equipment, the taxpayer must recapture, as ordinary income, the MACRS deduction, including any Section 179 deduction (discussed as follows), up to the amount realized on the equipment disposition.

Expensing

Under IRC section 179, an equipment owner can elect to deduct (expense) currently up to 1,000,000 U.S. dollars of MACRS property (excluding some types of property, such as property used predominately outside of the United States) used in the active conduct of its business in a tax year (the 1,000,000 U.S. dollar limit is the total per taxpayer, not for each equipment item). For tax years starting after 2018, these limitations are subject to adjustment for inflation. Additionally, there are other technical requirements that may come into play, so Section 179 must be reviewed in its entirety before making the election.

Summary

There are two key tax benefits that an equipment owner has available: equipment depreciation and, currently for certain energy property, an energy tax credit for new equipment. Each tax benefit in effect adds to the profitability of a lease investment through tax offsets available.

CHAPTER 12

Understanding the Tax Lease Rules

The True Lease

If the tax attributes discussed in Chapter 11 for a lease are important to a product vendor, as a lessor, then it is important that the contract in fact qualify as a *true* lease for federal income tax purposes. And, if a lease qualifies as a true lease for tax purposes, the lessee customer can deduct its lease payment as an expense for income tax purposes. If a lease does not qualify as a true lease for income tax purposes, the lessee is deemed to be the equipment owner for income tax purposes (and can claim the equipment ownership tax benefits), the lessor cannot claim the equipment ownership tax benefits, and the lessee cannot deduct the lease payments as a rent expense.

Taking this another step further, if a product vendor is unable to timely use any available equipment ownership tax benefits, because, for example, they have a loss carry forward, it should consider, for example, selling the transaction to a third-party financing company that can use the tax benefits. In this case, the product vendor will want to ensure that the lease with its customer is, in fact, a true lease for income tax purposes; otherwise, those benefits will be lost by the third-party financing company, and the customer will forfeit the rent deductions.

What, then, characterizes a lease as a *true* lease for income tax purposes? The term is not specifically defined as such in the Internal Revenue Code or its underlying regulations. Two U.S. Supreme Court cases, however, established basic definitional rules—*Helvering v. F. and R. Lazarus and Co.*, 308 U.S. 252 (1939) and *Frank Lyon Company v. United States*, 435 U.S. 561 (1978). The *Helvering* case set down a substance over form rule—that the tax nature of what is purported to be a true lease depends on whether the lessor can be determined to have sufficient property ownership of the asset involved, taking into account all the surrounding facts and circumstances, to be accorded the tax attributes available to an asset owner, or whether the purported lessor is really a conditional seller, an option holder, a lender, or some other type of transaction participant. The case's decision was the basic guidance looked to until, in 1978, the advent of the *Frank Lyon* case, when the U.S. Supreme Court took another look at the leasing tax ownership issue and advanced in considering tax ownership, and therefore, true lease status, that to determine if the lessor, rather than the lessee, is the equipment's tax owner, was whether the lessor had "significant and genuine attributes of the traditional lessor status," which attributes were, in any particular case, to be dependent on the facts.

While the ultimate *true* lease test is based on the transaction's facts and circumstances, the Internal Revenue Service (IRS), in 1975, provided guidelines for leveraged lease transactions (transactions financed in part with third-party debt), which, if followed, will help assure the true lease nature. In the form of four published Revenue Procedures (Revenue Procedure 75–21, Revenue Procedure 75–28, Revenue Procedure 76–30, and Revenue Procedure 79–48), collectively called the *Guidelines,* the IRS set out the formal criteria that must be met if the parties to a transaction want to obtain a ruling (referred to as a private letter ruling) from the IRS that the transaction qualifies as a lease for federal income tax purposes. Revenue Procedure 75–21, which contained the *foundation* rules for obtaining a favorable opinion from the IRS that a transaction would qualify as a *true* lease for federal income tax purposes, was refined and reissued by a later Revenue Procedure, Revenue Procedure 2001–28, which, together with Revenue Procedure 2001–29, now comprise what are referred to as the *Guidelines*. While nominally limited to ruling requests (when the IRS is formally asked for an opinion), the *Guidelines* provide helpful guidance on achieving true lease status even where the parties to the transaction do not request an IRS private letter ruling and even if the lease is not a leveraged lease, where the lessor borrows a portion of the cost of the equipment from a third-party lender. Additionally, industry practice is that even if a lease is not a leveraged lease, to the extent that the *Guidelines* may apply, they are generally followed.

Prior to the issuance of the *Guidelines*, the parities to a lease transaction found some guidance in Revenue Ruling 55–540 (1955–2 CB 39), discussed later in this chapter. Revenue Ruling 55–540, which still has guidance applicability, focuses primarily on the describing aspects of a transaction that would cause it to fail to qualify as a true lease. It has applicability to *all* purported lease transactions, not just *leveraged* lease transactions.

Ensuring True Lease Treatment

How do the parties maximize their chances of obtaining true lease status? The best two alternatives—obtain an IRS private ruling letter or proceed without one while following the *Guidelines, as applicable* and Revenue Ruling 55–540.

Getting an IRS Private Letter Ruling

As a general matter, if a taxpayer submits a ruling request to the IRS concerning a transaction, the IRS, after reviewing the request, will rule on some or all the transaction's tax consequences. Provided the information submitted was accurate and complete, if the transaction parties receive a favorable ruling from the IRS, they can rest assured that the transaction's anticipated tax results will not be challenged. It should be noted, however, that even if all the *Guidelines* are not met, the IRS will still consider a favorable ruling that a transaction qualifies as a true lease in appropriate cases based on all the facts and circumstances. While the safest route is to obtain a ruling, it is typically not the optimum alternative for a number of reasons: preparing and submitting the request involves a significant amount of legal work resulting in a higher transaction cost, a fee must be paid to the IRS, submitting a request takes a considerable amount of time (both to prepare the request and for the IRS to rule), and if the IRS's ruling is unfavorable and the transaction has been closed, there is a risk that this will draw attention to an issue that may otherwise have gone unnoticed.

Following the IRS Tax Lease Rules

When an IRS letter ruling is not practical, the next safest approach is to structure a lease transaction so it complies with the IRS's *Guidelines* to the extent they apply, understanding the *Guidelines* were designed to address leases structured as leveraged leases. Although, the *Guidelines* do not establish as a matter a law whether a transaction will or will not qualify as a true lease, as a practical matter, it is highly unlikely that a transaction meeting the *Guidelines* would have IRS audit problems.

The IRS Tax Guidelines

As aforementioned, Revenue Procedure 75–21 was modified and superseded by Revenue Procedure 2001–28. Revenue Procedure 2001–28 (CB 1156, 5/07/2001) generally sets out conditions that must be met for there to be an advance ruling on a leveraged lease, and Revenue Procedure 2001-29 (CB 2001–1 1160) sets out information and representations required to be furnished by taxpayers in a leveraged leasing transaction advance ruling request.

It is important to keep in mind that even though the *Guidelines* apply only to leveraged leases, as stated earlier, the parties to a non-leveraged transaction are well advised to consider those portions of the *Guidelines*, discussed as follows, that apply to the transaction aspects. In addition to following the *Guidelines*, prospective lessors and lessees will want to comply with Revenue Ruling 55–540 (1955–2 CB 39), explained as follows, which gives some general guidance on all types of leasing transactions, leveraged and non-leveraged.

A *true* lease checklist has been included in the Appendix.

Minimum Investment Requirements

Under the *Guidelines,* the lessor must initially make an unconditional equity investment, referred to as the *minimum investment*, in the equipment equal to at least 20 percent of its cost. This can be done in a variety of ways: with cash, with other consideration, or by assuming the obligation to buy the equipment. The unconditional nature requirement is to prevent the lessor from arranging to receive, either from the lessee or certain lessee-related parties, all or any part of its equity investment back once the equipment is put into service.

The lessor must also maintain this 20 percent *minimum investment* in the equipment during the lease term. The minimum investment test must also be met at the end of the lease term, that is, the lessor must show that the leased equipment's estimated fair market residual value is equal to at least 20 percent of its original cost, and that a reasonable estimate of the equipment's useful life at the end of the lease term is the longer of one year or 20 percent of the equipment's originally estimated useful life. This is usually validated by obtaining an appraisal of what the equipment will be valued at lease end.

Transaction Profit Requirements

The *Guidelines* provide that the lessor must make a profit on the transaction. Simply, the lessor must be able to show that the lease transaction makes economic sense without considering the tax benefits. Not only must a lessor anticipate a profit, they must also demonstrate that the transaction will produce a positive cash flow that is *reasonable* in amount, that is, essentially, the rents and other required lessee payments must comfortably exceed the aggregate outflows.

No Lessee Investment

Generally, the lessee cannot invest in the equipment by providing funds necessary to buy, add to, modify, or improve the equipment.

The Lessee Cannot be a Lender

Under the *Guidelines,* the lessee and members of the lessee group, such as affiliated companies, are specifically prohibited from lending funds to the lessor to assist in equipment financing. Thus, direct loans and other credit-extending techniques like those described in the previous subsection will transgress the *Guidelines* and prevent the issuance of a favorable private ruling on the transaction.

Certain Guarantees Cannot be Used

The lessee and certain lessee-associated parties, such as their parent company or sister subsidiary, cannot guarantee any equipment debt. Lessee-related parties, however, can guarantee the conventional obligations found in a net lease, such as rent, maintenance, or insurance premium obligations.

Any Lessee Purchase Options must be at Fair Market Value

To ensure that the lessee is not the equipment owner, the *Guidelines* prohibit any arrangement granting a lessee or lessee-related party the option to buy the leased equipment at a price below its fair market value. This rule essentially eliminates all low, or nominal, fixed price purchase options, such as one dollar purchase options.

The Lessor Cannot have the Right to Require an Equipment Sale

A lessor is specifically prohibited from having any initial right to require *any party* to buy the leased equipment for any reason, except when there are nonconformities with written supply, construction, or manufacture specifications, thus eliminating so-called *put options*, an ability to force an equipment sale at a predetermined price at the lease term's end to, for example, the lessee, a manufacturer, or an equipment dealer. For a lessor concerned about whether certain equipment will have any residual value at the end of the lease term, this is a risk it must assess.

Uneven Rents must Meet Certain Tests

Step rentals, such as *low-high* or *high-low* rent structures must meet certain guidelines. Uneven rents payments may be subject to Internal Revenue Code Section 467, and related regulations, with Internal Revenue Code Section 1.467–3(c)(4) providing an uneven rent test, it being specifically stated in the *Guidelines*, whether or not the uneven rent test is met will not affect a taxpayer's ability to obtain an advance ruling that a true lease exists. Section 467 provides for determining how uneven rents will be treated for federal income tax purposes.

Limited-Use Property

To obtain a favorable ruling, it is necessary to establish that it is commercially feasible for a party, not the lessee or a member of the lessee group, to lease or buy the property from the lessor—demonstrating that it is not limited use property. Limited-use property is property not expected to be useful to, or usable by, the lessor except for purposes of continued leasing or transfer to the lessee or a member of the lessee group so, in effect, the lessee will receive the equipment's ownership benefits for substantially its entire useful life.

What must an IRS Private Letter Ruling Request Contain?

In submitting a ruling request to the IRS, the taxpayer must present the information the *Guidelines* require in the manner prescribed by Revenue Procedure 2001–28, as modified by Revenue Procedure 2001–29. Generally, all the parties to the transaction, including the lessor and the lessee, must join in the ruling request. The request must contain a summary of the surrounding facts. The request must be accompanied by certain relevant documents, such as the lease, any economic analysis, prospectus, or other document used to induce the lessor to invest (if the transaction was brokered), the type and quality of the leased equipment, whether the equipment is new, reconstructed, used, or rebuilt, when, how, and where the equipment will be, or was, first placed in service or use, whether the equipment will be permanently or temporarily attached to land, buildings, or other property, and the flow of funds among the parties. Additionally, the request must disclose the lease term, and any renewals or extensions, and any purchase and sale options.

The Foundation Tax Rules

Two decades before issuing the initial *Guidelines,* the IRS issued Revenue Ruling 55–540 (1955–12 CB 39) detailing the factors that it considered in deciding whether a leasing transaction is really a conditional sale for tax purposes. Unlike the current *Guidelines,* Revenue Ruling 55–540 sets out the IRS audit position, rather than dealing with what is required to obtain a ruling. This ruling, however, is much less useful than the *Guidelines* because it is less precise. But, by checking its tests, you will help assure a leasing transaction's tax viability.

In this ruling, the IRS stated generally that whether an agreement, which in form is a lease, is in substance a conditional sales contract depends upon the intent of the parties as evidenced by the provisions of the agreement, read in the light of the facts and circumstances existing at the time the agreement was executed.

The IRS then went on to state that an intent that would cause an arrangement to be treated as a sale instead of a lease for tax purposes is found if one or more of the following factors exist:

- Portions of the periodic payments are specifically made applicable to an equity interest to be acquired by the lessee.
- The lessee will acquire title to the property under lease on the payment of a stated number of *rentals* that the lessee under the contract must make.
- The total amount that the lessee must pay for a relatively short period of use constitutes an inordinately large proportion of the total sum required to acquire the title.
- The agreed *rental* payments materially exceed the current fair rental value.
- The property may be acquired by the lessee under a purchase option at a price that is nominal in relation to the property's value at the time the option may be exercised (determined at the time the agreement was entered into) or which is relatively small when compared to the total payments that the lessee must make.
- Some portion of the periodic payments is specifically designated as interest or is otherwise readily recognizable as the equivalent of interest.

It is interesting to note that Revenue Ruling 55–540 provides guidelines for determining whether a conditional sale contract exists. The assumption is that if a conditional sales contract does not exist and the parties structured the transaction as a tax lease, everyone is on safe ground. If the transaction is structurally complex, experienced tax leasing counsel may be necessary to get adequate assurances.

Summary

If the parties to a lease transaction intend to have the lease character-ized for tax purposes as a lease, they must know the tax rules governing whether a transaction will, in fact, be considered by the applicable taxing authorities as a *true* lease for tax purposes. If a lease is so considered, the lessor will be deemed to be the lease asset's owner and, thus, able to claim the available equipment ownership tax benefits. The lessee, on the other hand, will be entitled to deduct the lease rent payable as an expense on its income tax returns. Failure of the lease to so qualify can result in an unfortunate re-arranging of the tax attributes assumed to be available—and the potential of an economic loss for the lessor, and a less attractive arrangement for the lessee. To avoid this problem, the rules governing the tax characterization must be understood. Unfortunately, doing this is often an art, because the tax rules are not always precise or clearly discernable.

CHAPTER 13

The Equipment Leasing and Financing Laws Under the Uniform Commercial Code

Overview

A product vendor setting up an in-house financing activity must know the various state laws applicable to equipment financing, embodied in the Uniform Commercial Code (UCC) of each state, discussed as follows, to properly draft and address requirements for a lease or financing contract, and to protect the equipment financed from lessee or financing contract obligor creditors and other third-party claims. There are no applicable federal leasing or financing law statues, other than for aircraft, marine, and rail-related equipment.

The various state equipment leasing laws are embodied in Article 2A of the UCC, as adopted by each state and the District of Columbia. Article 2A was initially drafted as a model law by the National Conference of Commissioners on Uniform State Laws to resolve the many issues and inconsistencies when it was determined that uniformity in leasing rules would clearly benefit all parties to a lease transaction, was sent to the various states (including the District of Columbia) for consideration and enactment into law. In most cases, it was adopted into law with few changes. In the case of Article 2A, a product vendor should generally understand its provisions, knowing that they will not be able to avail themselves of the benefits of a special category of Article 2A *finance leases*, for reasons you will see next.

In addition to Article 2A, there are two additional and important UCC sections (also referred to as *Articles*) that can impact a product vendor equipment financing, Article 2 (Sales) and Article 9 (Secured Transactions; Sales of Accounts and Chattel Paper). These *Articles* existed prior to the formulation and adoption of Article 2A and were created to provide guidance, in part, for commercial and consumer sales, and the general financing of personal property. A detailed analysis of UCC Article 2 and Article 9, dealing with the sales of personal property, is beyond the scope of this book, but their essential elements will be examined so that you have a working knowledge of how they may come into play in an equipment lease or other financing situation.

This topic area is one that should be discussed with legal counsel to ensure it is fully understood based on how you, as a product vendor, set up your financing activity.

UCC Article 2, Sales: An Overview

UCC Article 2 establishes the rights and remedies of the parties to a product (personal property) sale transaction, which will be of concern to a product vendor, including a product vendor with an in-house financing activity. It imposes, for example, certain implied product warranties that a purchaser can enforce against a seller of goods, a product vendor, and something that will not affect a non-product vendor, such as an independent financing company. The best way to put Article 2 into perspective in relation to Article 2A is to understand how it differs from Article 2A, as Article 2A was, in part, based upon Article 2. Both *Articles* address personal property, basically parting company when the transaction is a lease financing (governed by Article 2A), as opposed to a straight product sale (governed by Article 2).

A few important commercial (non-consumer) aspects that Article 2A eliminated from the Article 2 sales rules are:

- Article 2A eliminated implied equipment warranties of equipment merchantability and fitness for use, existing in Article 2.
- Article 2A eliminated implied product infringement warranties when the lease qualifies as a *finance lease* under Article 2A.

UCC Article 9, Secured Transactions; Sales of Accounts and Chattel Paper: An Overview

UCC Article 9 governs secured lending transactions, transactions in which the parties intend to create a security interest in the personal property (such as equipment) financed under, for example, a conditional sale or other loan financing arrangement. A security interest is simply an interest in personal property that secures the payment or performance of an obligation, in effect a lien on the personal property. If, for example, an equipment vendor lessor enters into a conditional sale arrangement (in effect, a loan) with an equipment vendor customer, a court would deem this type of lending transaction to be governed by the UCC Article 9 rules. And, in this case, a product vendor should obtain as collateral protection for the loan repayment obligations a security interest in the underlying equipment contract payments and the related equipment. UCC Article 9 would also come into play if a lease transaction turns out (even unintended by the parties) to, in substance, be a secured loan or what is something referred to as a *financing* (that is, not in fact a lease), such as when the lessee has a one dollar purchase option.

UCC Article 2A, Equipment Leasing: An Overview

Article 2A as originally proposed by its drafters has, as already suggested, been adopted by all the states (including the District of Columbia), with, in some cases, relatively minor modifications, and sets forth the legal guidelines for determining whether a transaction purporting to be a lease is a lease for state law purposes. Very simply, Article 2A is intended to govern the formation, construction, and enforceability of equipment lease contracts.

With a few exceptions, the Article 2A provisions can be overridden by agreement between the parties. The exceptions usually relate to matters of public policy and what would be considered not good faith dealings. For issues not addressed by the parties, Article 2A governs. In effect, for a lease transaction, Article 2A fills in aspects of the transaction that the parties did not explicitly cover in their contract.

Lease Distinguished from Security Interest

UCC Article 2A, along with Article 2 and Article 9, specifically defines the characteristics of leases, sales, and security interests. It is often not easy to determine if the transaction purporting to be a lease qualifying under Article 2A is, in fact, an Article 2A qualifying lease, or should instead be considered, under state law, a non-lease, or secured, financing.

Under Article 2A, a lease is essentially defined as a transfer of the right to possession and use of personal property for a period of time (term) in return for consideration (such as money), *unless* it is a *sale* or a *security interest*. Typically, the most difficult part in making an assessment is determining whether the transaction is a *security interest*. Although the definition of security interest spells out specific factors that will disqualify a transaction as a lease and cause it to be deemed a security interest, and factors that in and of themselves will not cause a purported lease to, in fact, be deemed a security interest, the definition also provides that the various transaction *facts and circumstances*, must be considered. The *facts and circumstances* benchmark is subject to interpretation, and thus can create characterization uncertainty.

Under UCC Article 2A, lease disqualifying factors are:

- the lease term equals or exceeds the remaining useful life of the equipment,
- the lessee is obligated to become the equipment owner at lease end or must renew the lease for the remaining economic useful life of the equipment,
- the lessee has the right to renew the equipment for a nominal amount (such as one dollar) or for no additional cost for the equipment's economic useful life, or
- the lessee has the right to purchase the equipment for a nominal amount (such as one dollar) or can acquire the equipment without cost.

Factors that in and of themselves will not cause a purported lease transaction to be disqualified as a lease are:

- the lease is a net or full payout lease,
- the lease has equipment renewal or purchase options, non-nominal in amount, even if at a fixed price,

- the lease obligates the lessee to assume certain ownership responsibilities, such as the risk of equipment loss or the obligation to pay taxes, maintenance costs, and insurance fees, or
- the present value of the lease amounts to be paid by the lessee is equal to or greater than the fair market value of the equipment.

As a rule of thumb, if the lessor retains a meaningful economic interest in the end-of-lease value of the equipment (residual), notwithstanding a lessee's right to exclusive use (subject to a lessee lease default) of the equipment during the lease term, it is a lease. Otherwise, it will not be so considered and must be treated as a secured financing, such as a secured loan or an installment sale financing. For example, if the lessee can become the equipment owner for no additional, or nominal, consideration the transaction is not a lease under Article 2A.

Protecting a Lessor's Equipment Interest

If the transaction qualifies as a lease under Article 2A, the lessor is deemed the equipment owner and no other creditors can successfully claim superior rights to the equipment. If a transaction does not qualify as a lease under Article 2A, and it is deemed to be an equipment financing, it will typically be governed by Article 9 (Secured Transactions) and, possibly, Article 2 (Sales). If the transaction fails to qualify as an Article 2A lease, the Article 9 rules will likely govern and the party designated as the lessor has to generally make certain initial and follow-up document filings (referred to as UCC statement filings) and, possibly, take certain other actions, to protect its equipment interest against third-party creditors of the lessee.

Notwithstanding the fact that lessors entering into Article 2A qualifying leases need not take any such protective UCC filing action, most lessors, as a matter of course, make what is referred to as an information-only (precautionary) filing using a UCC-1 Financing Statement form. Simply, the lessor files a typical UCC-1 financing statement against the lessee, with a notice typed or printed in the body of the UCC-1 financing statement indicating that it is an information-only filing.

A UCC-1 financing statement is a standard form that must be used and filed in the appropriate jurisdiction where the obligor is organized and on which the various party names and addresses are listed along with an equipment description.

What are the Practical Implications of a Lease being Deemed a Secured Financing?

If a court determines that a transaction purporting to be an equipment lease for state law purposes is, in fact, a secured financing, UCC Article 9 comes into play. And, if the rules of Article 9 are not complied with, a lessor could lose their secured position, that is, their ability to claim a superior right in the equipment over that of other lessee creditors who may have an effective claim to that equipment because of certain security interest rights they have in a lessee's assets. If this occurs, a court may in effect take the position that, notwithstanding that the agreement is labeled a lease, the transaction is the functional equivalent of an equipment installment, or conditional sale or a loan, financing arrangement.

A Key Lease Concept Under Article 2A: The Finance Lease

To recognize the economic and business realties in certain types of equipment financings, UCC Article 2A has a special category of lease, referred to as a *finance lease*, which has special lessor benefits. For a lease to quality as an Article 2A finance lease, and be automatically entitled to the unique benefits offered under Article 2A, the lease must meet the following criteria:

- the lessor must not select, manufacture, or supply the equipment,
- the lessor must acquire the equipment in connection with the lease (that means, not out of inventory), and
- the lessee must be provided information, before lease execution, about what equipment warranties are provided, who stands behind them, and what remedy limitations or modifications exist.

The key advantages for a lessor in having a transaction classified for UCC purposes as an Article 2A statutory finance lease are:

- there are no lessor-implied equipment warranties of fitness and merchantability, as may be provided in other lease transactions, and
- the lessee's rent payment obligation is deemed to be an irrevocable commercial lessee obligation to pay rents, that is, the rent payment obligation under a lease classified as an Article 2A finance lease is automatically deemed to be a statutory hell or high-water obligation (rents are non-cancelable and absolutely and unconditionally payable, and not capable of being offset or otherwise reduced, even though not specifically stated as such in the lease contract).

A key advantage to a lessee in a finance lease transaction is that Article 2A automatically passes through the equipment seller's warranties (subject to any warranty exclusions) to the lessee.

Lessor Lease Remedies Under Article 2A

In a lessee lease default situation, the courts had been uniformly inconsistent and, at times incorrect, in determining what damages a lessor was entitled to receive. In keeping with its philosophy, Article 2A addressed this critical issue by allowing the lessors and lessees to generally contractually agree in the lease contract on what default and remedy standards would apply. Article 2A does, however, provide safe harbor provisions that would apply if the lease contract default or remedy provisions were either invalid or omitted. Under Article 2A, unless so stated in the lease contract, the lessor:

- does not have to give notice of default or enforcement action, and
- can terminate the lease, repossess the equipment, sell or otherwise dispose of the equipment, and recover damages for breach of the contract.

Lessee Lease Remedies Under Article 2A

Article 2A provides for lessee remedies if the lessor is in default under a lease contract, which, unless otherwise *drafted out* of the lease contract, will apply. Depending on the type of breach, for example, the lessee may seek to cancel the lease contract, reject the equipment, revoke its acceptance of the nonconforming equipment, enforce specific performance as to the equipment, seek to recover rents or other payments made (such as a security deposit), or pursue other damages that would typically flow from a contract breach. Because of this, typically, lessors add a lease provision in which the lessee waives its Article 2A remedies. If the lease, however, is an Article 2A statutory finance lease, the lessee may not, other than as stated earlier, cancel the lease, or offset any amounts that may be due to the lessee against the rents payable.

A Consumer Lease Under Article 2A

Although beyond the scope of this chapter, it is important to keep in mind that Article 2A makes a distinction between commercial lease transactions and consumer lease transactions, providing for added protections to a consumer lessee. Generally, a consumer lease is defined as "a lease that a lessor regularly engaged in the business of leasing or selling makes to a lessee who is an individual and who takes under the lease primarily for a personal, family, or household purpose." Under the various state Article 2A enactments, you will find, typically, that the total lease contract rent payments, excluding equipment purchase or lease renewal option payments, may not exceed a certain legislature-specified amount.

Summary

As discussed, over the years, the courts have often struggled with whether an equipment financing transaction should be characterized as a lease, or as a conditional, or installment, sale for state law purposes. There are no federal financing law statues, other than for aircraft, marine, and rail-related equipment. UCC Article 2A, adopted by all states and the District of Columbia to address equipment financing inconsistencies, contains the various jurisdictional equipment leasing laws. In addition to Article 2A, there are two additional and important UCC *Articles* that can impact an equipment financing, Article 2 (Sales) and Article 9 (Secured Transactions; Sales of Accounts and Chattel Paper).

CHAPTER 14

An Equipment Financing Trend: Managed Services and Fee-Per-Use Agreements

Managed Services and Fee-Per-Use Agreements: A New Equipment Financing Product Trend

Although not a traditional financing contract arrangement, equipment provided by a product vendor in connection with what are referred to as managed services agreements and fee-per-use agreements is a relatively recent offering trend. These agreement forms enable a product vendor to build in extra profit items, offer expanded services, and are typically favorably viewed by vendor customers. There are, however, financing challenges in using these types of agreements, as discussed next.

The Concept and Structure of a Managed Services Agreement

A managed services agreement generally provides a customer with bundled equipment and services for an agreed-upon term, ranging from five to 20 years. Managed services agreements are often used with energy-saving offerings where the services provider provides energy-saving equipment and related services, such as maintenance, as well as other collateral services, for a bundled stated price, but they are also increasingly used in connection with providing technology and medical equipment and related services. Customers favor this type of agreement because there is a possibility the payment obligations will be treated as off-balance sheet obligations if the new accounting rules, discussed in Chapter 8, do not dictate otherwise and, accordingly, if treated as an off-balance sheet item, the contract will not adversely affect their financial ratios for borrowing purposes. For the customer, using third-party services providers can eliminate, or reduce, the needs for internal service staffing.

The Concept and Structure of a Fee-Per-Use Agreement

A fee-per-use agreement is another potentially *off-balance sheet* service-type contract gaining popularity, particularly in the medical field, assuming, again, that the new accounting rules, discussed in Chapter 8, do not dictate otherwise. Under this type of contract, the product vendor typically supplies a customer with the product vendor's equipment for an agreed-upon term and imposes a charge for the equipment generally on the basis of the amount of supplies or disposables used in connection with the equipment operation, often obligating the customer to a minimum periodic supply or disposable use over the contract term.

Pricing Managed Services Agreement and Fee-Per-Use Agreement Payments

As stated, typically, a managed services agreement has a bundled price where all listed equipment and services are incorporated into one periodic payment, the total of which covers the services provider's overhead and invested costs, with a profit. At times, however, the various service components are broken down into separate payment obligations listed for each component. When there is a bundled payment, the services provider is attempting to make it difficult for the customer to determine the cost, including any finance charge, of any one item, such as for the equipment, being supplied, thus preventing the customer from easily, if at all, being able to determine whether its offering is competitive for any one component.

In structuring the managed services agreement periodic payments, the services provider typically attempts to determine what the periodic payment must be to pay for the services offered as well as to fully amortize the cost of equipment provided over the contract term, minus any end-of-contract-term equipment value. For a product vendor, developing a managed services financing product can be a solid marketing strategy.

As with managed services agreements, fee-per-use agreements also often attempt to disguise specific charges used to pay the full costs of what is being provided, such as any equipment. For example, it is not unusual for a fee-per-use agreement to charge a fee based on each time the equipment is used for, say, a procedure-referred to as a *fee-per-use* or simply a *fee-per* charge. In that case, there are, typically, a minimum number of uses the customer must guarantee to the services provider during the use period resulting in a minimum monthly or annual charge. The number of uses is often measured by the product vendor through equipment embedded software remotely accessed.

In structuring the fee-per charge, the service provider typically determines what the minimum fee-per-use charge must be to cover the disposables supplied, as well as to fully amortize the cost of equipment provided over the contract term, minus any end-of-contract-term equipment value. Any annual aggregate minimum per-use charge is often set at an amount that is less than the customer's historical annual use. This approach may, again assuming the new accounting rules do not dictate otherwise, achieve off-balance sheet treatment for the payment obligation, a result not readily achievable if the equipment were subject to a lease running for the same period. For a product vendor, a fee-per-use financing product can also be a solid marketing strategy.

The Advantages and Risks for a Product Vendor in Using Fee-Per-Use and Managed Services Agreements

Product vendors supplying services on a bundled basis with equipment can often build in higher profit margins than they are usually able to by simply supplying equipment because the bundled charges, as stated earlier, make it difficult, if not impossible, and price compare and shop its competitors. The risk in using these types of contracts, as also stated earlier, is that they may be easily cancelable before the contracted term end by the customer, discussed next, and, in addition, can present contract financing challenges for a product vendor.

Financing Challenges for Managed Services and Fee-Per-Use Agreements

The challenge in using managed services agreements is that they typically do not contain a firm, non-cancelable payment commitment, referred to as a hell or high-water payment obligation found in net finance leases, discussed in Chapter 9 and, even if they did, any non-cancelable provision enforceability would be likely questionable because if the services provider breaches its contract service obligations, it is unlikely a court would enforce any of the customer future payment obligations. Added to that issue is the fact that some managed services agreements allow customer agreement cancelation *for convenience,* which means, basically, any time during the contract term the customer decides they no longer want or need the equipment or services. As a result, a product vendor may be prevented from selling this type of contract or otherwise accessing receivable loan financing from a third-party financing company for this type of contract, unless the product vendor gives an indemnity or a buyback commitment to the purchaser or financing party for any termination for convenience or customer termination based on a claim of breach of the services or equipment obligations before the end of the contract term. Accordingly, this becomes a product vendor credit issue, with the lender or the third-party financing company looking to the services provider's creditworthiness to support its non-performance indemnity or buyback commitment.

Although a fee-per-use agreement may contain terms and conditions like those found in a lease agreement, including a full payment hell or high-water payment obligation and equipment insurance requirements, there are still third-party financing challenges. An included hell or high-water payment obligation is an effort to use an approach that works in a lease to assure that the payment obligation can be financed through a third-party lender, but its enforceability may still be subject to challenge if any services or supplies collateral to the equipment are not provided or are otherwise defective. Accordingly, and notwithstanding any hell or high-water payment provision, a fee-per-use agreement may still be subject to customer cancelation based on a customer claim of services or supplier obligation breach, which can prevent a product vendor from selling this type of contract to, or borrowing against its contract receivables from, a third-party finance company, unless the product vendor gives an indemnity or a buyback commitment to the purchaser or financing party for any customer claim of product vendor breach of its contract obligations before the end of the contract term.

The structuring of any managed services or fee-per-use contract indemnity or buyback commitment can be challenging. In effect, it may result in a product vendor being obligated to buy back the contract if the customer cancels the contract for any reason prior to the end of the financing term. This may create an accounting issue for a product vendor if they want to *book* (record for financial reporting purposes) the full revenues received from the contract sale or the discounting of the payment stream at the time of the financing transaction, something that it will need agreement on from its accountants. The accountants may determine the amount received from the financing is subject to a significant recourse contingency and, accordingly, the cash received may not be capable of being fully accounted for, booked, at the time of payment, requiring a partial booking upfront, with the remainder being booked over the term of the contract. Setting up the indemnity carefully, however, may allow the vendor to book their full revenues at the time of assignment if, for example, the indemnity is triggered for a customer payment stoppage as a result of a customer credit problem, such as bankruptcy, and not for a failure by the vendor to properly perform its service obligations. These indemnities are often highly negotiated and finely tuned, but properly written can give the third-party lender or financing company purchaser assurances that the service provider's credit stands behind the equipment repayment obligations except for a customer credit problem—basically, a risk the equipment financing company typically takes in any financing transaction.

Summary

To address the adverse consequences for their customers of various accounting implications requiring on-balance sheet treatment of long-term liabilities in connection with lease contracts providing equipment or to add additional profits, a product vendor should consider offering managed services or fee-per-use agreements, where equipment and collateral products, such as software, supplies, or equipment maintenance, can be bundled in a customer offering. The accounting and reporting of these types of agreements can have many challenges and requires a detailed analysis of the obligations and commitments, both for the equipment user and for the service provider. In each case, the services provider's credit strength may be a factor in obtaining financing for the cost of the equipment being provided under a services or fee-per-use arrangement.

CHAPTER 15

The Bankruptcy Rules

Overview

Inevitably, if you, as a product vendor, are involved in an equipment financing transaction, you will, at some time, be involved in a customer bankruptcy proceeding. So, an understanding of the bankruptcy rules is essential. This chapter will examine the basic provisions of the federal bankruptcy law (the law under which most bankruptcies are handled), known as the Bankruptcy Code. The Bankruptcy Code is embodied in Title 11 of the U.S. Code. An examination of similar state laws will not be addressed because they are rarely encountered in an equipment lease or financing situation.

The impact on a product vendor in the role of a lessor, and any equipment lender to the product vendor lessor, if a lessee files for protection under, or is involuntarily subjected to, the bankruptcy laws can be significant. The same is true for any other type of equipment financing. For the equipment lessor or financing party, an understanding of the Bankruptcy Code rules is necessary to properly assess whether to enter into an equipment lease or other financing contract, to properly draft the financing contract, to facilitate a better potential recovery, and to know what it can and cannot do when a bankruptcy occurs.

Basically, there are two types of proceedings in bankruptcy, reorganization proceedings and liquidation proceedings. A reorganization proceeding is one in which a company in financial difficulty, referred to in bankruptcy as the debtor, has elected to avail itself of bankruptcy protection to get some breathing room from its creditors to see if it can restructure its business and get financially back on track. A liquidation proceeding is one in which it has been determined that a debtor can no longer continue in business. In a liquidation proceeding, the debtor's assets are liquidated (generally, sold off) for the benefit of the debtor's creditors. A bankruptcy liquidation or reorganization proceeding can be voluntary, one in which the debtor seeks bankruptcy law protection or assistance, or one in which the debtor is involuntarily forced into bankruptcy by its creditors.

There are, for a lessor, two key Bankruptcy Code provisional concepts that should be highlighted here because they govern two important practical aspects of a lessee-in-bankruptcy lease transaction. The first is the automatic stay provision found in Bankruptcy Code Section 362, which puts a hold on important lessor actions once bankruptcy occurs. The second are the provisions, found in Bankruptcy Code Section 265, which permit the rejection or assumption of an unexpired lease by or on behalf of a lessee in bankruptcy. Also worthy of mention, for aircraft, railroad rolling stock, and vessel lessors, there are two additional sections that can be important, Bankruptcy Code Section 1110 and Section 1168, which allow certain equipment preference repossession rights, discussed in greater detail as follows.

Bankruptcy Liquidation and Reorganization

There are five bankruptcy chapter proceedings, Bankruptcy Code Chapters 7, 9, 11, 12, and 13, that cover the various types of liquidation or reorganization (sometimes referred to as restructuring) proceedings available. Bankruptcy Chapter 7 proceedings govern individual and entity liquidations. Bankruptcy Chapter 11 proceedings govern individual business entrepreneurs (as well certain other individuals) and entity reorganizations. Chapters 7 and 11 are the ones typically encountered or used when commercial lease transactions are involved. Bankruptcy Chapter 9 governs municipal bankruptcies, Bankruptcy Chapter 12 governs family farmer reorganization proceedings, and Bankruptcy Chapter 13 governs certain limited individual (typically non-business) reorganizations. The later three chapter proceedings are not typically encountered in the day-to-day business of equipment leasing and lending and will be left to your reading if such a situation arises.

Chapter 7, Liquidation: An Overview

A Bankruptcy Code Chapter 7 proceeding, one in which the business assets are liquidated for the benefit of the business creditors, is the most difficult one for an equipment lessor or lender because it is likely that the lessor or lender will incur a significant economic loss. In a Chapter 7 proceeding, if granted, the individual debtor gets a complete discharge from all debts. Although the substantive effect is the same for an entity liquidation proceeding, technically, when an entity is involved, such as a corporation, an actual formal discharge from all debts is not granted, but the business entity is expected to dissolve its existence under the applicable non-bankruptcy laws, after its assets are liquidated. In general, as aforementioned, both business entities and individuals can request (a voluntary proceeding initiated by the debtor) or, depending on the circumstances, be forced into a Chapter 7 liquidation (an involuntary proceeding initiated by one or more the debtor's creditors).

Once the debtor (such as an equipment lessee) files under Chapter 7 seeking the protection of the bankruptcy laws, an interim bankruptcy trustee is appointed through the bankruptcy court having jurisdiction over the proceeding. In some cases, the interim trustee may be replaced by a bankruptcy trustee who has been elected by the debtor's creditors. If the debtor's creditors do not elect their trustee, the interim trustee will in effect become the final bankruptcy trustee.

The job of the bankruptcy trustee is to determine the proper disposition (liquidation) of the debtor's assets. In some cases, the assets will be sold to third parties and the proceeds distributed to the debtor's creditors in accordance with certain priority rules mentioned as follows. If the creditor is a secured creditor, such as an equipment lender with a valid lien on certain assets of the debtor, typically, their rights to the secured collateral are retained. Some assets considered inconsequential or burdensome may simply be abandoned by the trustee and returned to the debtor. Certain assets may be exempt and will be out of the trustee's reach.

Chapter 11, Reorganization: An Overview

A Bankruptcy Code Chapter 11 proceeding can be commenced voluntarily by the debtor, or involuntarily against the debtor by certain creditors of the debtor. As suggested earlier, the intent behind a Chapter 11 proceeding is to facilitate the reorganization of the debtor to put the debtor fully back on its financial feet and, thus, prevent it from falling into a Chapter 7 liquidation. If a Chapter 11 reorganization is unsuccessful, a Chapter 7 proceeding is assuredly next.

In a Chapter 11 proceeding, it is not unusual for the debtor (such as an equipment lessee), as opposed to a trustee, to retain control over the business assets, in which case, the debtor is referred to as the debtor-in-possession, or the DIP. A trustee, however, may be appointed through the bankruptcy court if there are grounds for doing so, typically, referred to as *for cause*.

The DIP, or trustee, if elected, is required to formulate a plan of reorganization, which must be approved by the governing bankruptcy court (subject to input from the creditors) in which the debtor is to pay their debts in accordance with the reorganization plan. The plan, if approved by the bankruptcy court, will typically, in effect, modify the payment responsibilities of the debtor, thus giving the debtor a new start going forward. As you may suspect, in a Chapter 11 proceeding, typically all the assets are not liquidated, but rather many are retained to facilitate the ongoing business operation. Under a Chapter 11 proceeding, however, assets are permitted to be liquidated to the extent necessary to ensure that the business, for example, survives. Equipment leases, as you will see next, among certain other asset transactions, receive special treatment.

Automatic Stay

An important concept within the Bankruptcy Code is something referred to as an automatic stay, provided for in Bankruptcy Code Section 362(c). Very simply, once bankruptcy is instituted, all actions against the bankrupt (debtor) are prohibited. This, for example, means that once the automatic stay exists (at the time bankruptcy is instituted), an equipment lessor cannot go in and get the leased equipment without the debtor's consent or court authority. The automatic stay also puts a stop to any potential legal proceedings that might be used to recover on any pre-bankruptcy petition claims against the debtor. The intent of the automatic stay is to protect the debtor and the bankruptcy estate's creditors from the item-by-item dismemberment of the estate's assets. Any knowing violation of the automatic stay rule will subject a lessor to actual and punitive damages.

Equipment Lease Treatment in Bankruptcy

Equipment leases are treated under the bankruptcy rules in a special manner. Section 365(a) of the Bankruptcy Code allows a bankruptcy trustee or a DIP to assume or reject all executory contracts, which include unexpired equipment lease contracts. Basically, an executory contract under contract law is a contract in which the obligations of all parties, in the case of a lease, the lessee and the lessor, are so unperformed that it would be considered a material contract breach if any party failed to meet its obligations giving the other party or parties a legal excuse not to perform its obligations.

Assumption or Rejection

If the equipment lease is assumed, the debtor's assets are deemed to be available for servicing (technically, the bankruptcy estate becomes bound by) the remaining lease obligations assumed. You might wonder whether, if the lessee is in bankruptcy, this is worth anything to a lessor. In fact, it is. To begin with, for the trustee or DIP to be able to assume the lease, the bankruptcy estate must do three things:

1. cure any lease default or provide adequate assurance that the default will be promptly cured,
2. pay the lessor for any default damages or provide adequate assurance that the default damages will be promptly paid, and
3. give adequate assurance that the future lease obligations will be met.

The real advantage to a lease assumption is that the lease payment obligations become a bankruptcy estate administration expense, giving the lessor a payment distribution priority over the claims of unsecured creditors for any damages arising for lease contract defaults following the assumption. To give you a priority preference perspective, in general, bankruptcy claims are treated in specified categories of priority. The secured claims are paid first, and the unsecured claims are paid next, with the equity owners taking the last recovery position. The assumption of a lease by the debtor requires the approval of the bankruptcy court, after notice, and an opportunity to be heard is given to the unsecured creditors, who may be hurt by the payment priority.

Interestingly, the typical event of default provision found in most lease contracts, such as lessee insolvency, a material adverse change in the lessee's financial condition, the commencement of a lessee bankruptcy proceedings, or the appointment of a trustee in bankruptcy for a lessee, are not *defaults* that must be cured as part of the lease assumption.

As stated earlier, the equipment lease can also be rejected, allowing the debtor to abandon any assets that the trustee or the DIP would in their reasonable business judgment consider burdensome to the bankruptcy estate. The decision, however, must be on an all or none basis (that is, if assumed, all the obligations must be assumed), unless the lease contract contains agreements that can be separated.

If the lease is rejected, however, the rejection is deemed to be a breach of the lease contract, and the lessor can not only reclaim their equipment, but it can make a claim in bankruptcy for any damages that have been incurred under the lease contract before the filing of the bankruptcy petition. The claim for damages would be a general unsecured claim. Once rejected, the lease cannot be assumed, even if it would be beneficial to the bankruptcy estate to do so.

The Assumption or Rejection Period

In a bankruptcy liquidation proceeding (Bankruptcy Code Chapter 7), the debtor (through the trustee in bankruptcy, if one is appointed) must decide whether to make the lease assumption or rejection within 60 days following the institution of the bankruptcy proceeding. If the decision to assume or reject is not made within the 60-day period, the lease contract is deemed to have been rejected. The 60-day period may be subject to extension by the bankruptcy court if it determines there is a valid reason to do so, often referred to as *for cause*. In the case of a Chapter 7 liquidation proceeding, unless the lease would have some value to the bankruptcy estate, such as for the unsecured creditors, which generally is unlikely, it would not be assumed.

In a bankruptcy reorganization (Bankruptcy Code Chapters 9, 11, 12, or 13), the rule is different. The debtor is allowed (through the trustee in bankruptcy, if one is appointed) to determine whether they want to assume or reject an equipment lease at any time, as long as the decision is made before the bankruptcy court puts it stamp of approval (referred to as *confirms*) the plan of reorganization. This decision time period, again, is subject to shortening upon notice to, and a hearing by, the bankruptcy court. In certain cases, it is possible for the bankruptcy court to approve a reorganization plan that permits the debtor to assume or reject an equipment lease after the reorganization has been approved by the court and is effective.

If an equipment lease is assumed in the reorganization proceeding, the general feeling is that it can still be rejected in a subsequent liquidation preceding (if the reorganization is not successful) or, possibly, if a trustee was appointed if the DIP was later thrown out by the bankruptcy court.

Special Treatment for Aircraft, Railroad Rolling Stock, and Vessels

As mentioned earlier, the Bankruptcy Code provides certain additional protections, under Bankruptcy Code Sections 1110 and 1168, for lessors of aircraft, railroad rolling stock, and vessels. Very simply, if the lessee or debtor wants to continue to use such equipment, they must cure all lease defaults that exist at the time of the filing of the bankruptcy proceeding, within 60 days following its filing; must timely perform all future obligations under the lease contract during the period of continued use, and, if a lease default occurs, must cure the default within 30 days following its occurrence. If these conditions are not met, the lessor can immediately repossess the equipment without regard to the Bankruptcy Code automatic stay provisions and without regard to any right the lessee would otherwise have under the Bankruptcy Code to use the equipment in the ordinary course of business (say, to assist in their ability to successfully come through a bankruptcy reorganization) or the powers of the bankruptcy court to stop (enjoin) any such repossession.

The commitment by the lessee or debtor, if they want to continue to hold this equipment, to cure past defaults and meet all ongoing obligations, however, is nothing more than an exception to the automatic stay, use of equipment and injunctive rules, which would otherwise come into play in a bankruptcy proceeding. It is not deemed to be an assumption of the entire lease contract, with the lessee debtor still able to terminate the lease arrangement when the equipment is no longer required. Whether, in fact, any right to repossess equipment is worth anything to a lessor, of course, depends on the value of the equipment at the time of repossession. If the value is not there, having the lessee or debtor continue to use the equipment may be the best alternative.

What Happens if the Lease is not a True Lease?

If an equipment lease turns out to, in fact, be a secured equipment financing (discussed in Chapter 13), for example, a security agreement or an installment (conditional) sale agreement, then the *lessor* can lose some benefits under bankruptcy, and its position is similar to the position of a secured creditor that provided a financing arrangement, which, in effect, is a loan. First, the *lease* does not have to be assumed or rejected by the debtor, and, second, and often of most concern, is that the debtor may be able to completely ignore the purported security interest in the equipment if the proper Uniform Commercial Code financing statement (a UCC-1) was not filed, was improperly filed, or certain other statutory requirements for *perfecting* the security interest in the equipment were not taken. In a pure bankruptcy liquidation proceeding, this reduces the lessor to that of an unsecured creditor.

In a bankruptcy reorganization proceeding, there are also adverse consequences. Even if proper Uniform Commercial Code filings were made, meaning that the equipment at hand was, in fact, successfully encumbered by the lessor's or financing party's security interest, there is no requirement under the Bankruptcy Code that any past defaults be cured by the debtor, nor does the debtor have to provide any comfort to a lessor or other financing party that it can adequately meet its payment or other obligations under the *lease*, or financing contract in order for it to continue to use the equipment. The debtor merely must give a lessor comfort, called *adequate protection*, that their security interest in the equipment will be secure. Worse yet for a lessor is that if the debtor wants to retain the equipment for use in a bankruptcy reorganization, the actual plan of reorganization may reduce the interest rate or payment terms originally agreed to under the purported lease contract, leaving the lessor with an unrecoverable deficiency. The *adequate protection* requirement is open for discussion in the bankruptcy court. It may, for example, take the form of a security deposit, the granting of a lien on additional assets the debtor has, or some form of payment preference over other bankruptcy creditors.

For those lessors who package maintenance or other equipment-related services with an equipment lease, if the lease is deemed to be, say, a conditional sale agreement, it is possible for the bankruptcy court to separate the two agreement arrangements, determining that the lessor is no longer the equipment owner, and treating the maintenance portion as an executory contract, allowing the debtor to assume or reject the equipment services. If the debtor decides to assume the services aspect, and the services were offered below the lessor's cost as part of the lease marketing inducement, the lessor may end up with an ongoing below-cost service responsibility.

Summary

The classification of an equipment lease as a true equipment lease for bankruptcy purposes has benefits. The debtor must decide whether to assume or reject a lease contract, giving the lessor some benefits over those of a typical secured or unsecured creditor in bankruptcy. If rejected, the lessor gets its equipment back and can file a bankruptcy claim as an unsecured creditor for the damages resulting from the lease rejection, deemed to be a contract breach. If the lease is assumed, the lessor has some assurance that they will be paid what is owed under the lease contract, subject to adjustment by the bankruptcy court. If a lease contract is not deemed to represent a true lease for bankruptcy purposes and, instead, is determined to be or, in fact, is, say, a security agreement or a conditional or installment sale arrangement, then, unless the lessor or financing party has taken the proper precaution under the Uniform Commercial Code to secure its interest in the equipment, it may lose the equipment collateral to the debtor and become an unsecured creditor.

Appendix

Suggested Additional Reference and Research Material:

Books:

The Handbook of Equipment Leasing, by Shawn D. Halladay and Sudhir P. Amenbal

Equipment Leasing, by Frank Fabozzi

Equipment Leasing – Leveraged Leasing, Fifth Edition, various authors, published by the Practicing Law Institute

The Complete Handbook of Equipment Leasing, Second Edition, 2015, Richard M. Contino, Esq., published by York House Press

Back Office Service Providers:

America Financial Services (www.greatamerica.com)

Orion First (www.orionfirst.com).

Business Sources:

First Lease Advisors (https://firstleaseadvisors.com)

Credit Assessment Products and Agencies:

Experian (https://experian.com)

PayNet (https://paynet.com)

Dunn and Bradstreet (https://dnb.com)

Hoovers (https://hoovers.com)

Equipment Leasing and Financing Industry Contacts:

Equipment Leasing and Finance Association (https://elfaonline.org/)

Financing Management and Processing Software:

Terra Vista Software (https://terravistasoftware.com)

Pricing Consultants:

Ivory Consulting Corporation, Walnut Creek, California
(https://ivorycc.com/)
Fairfield Capital Group, LLC (https://fairfieldcapital.net)

State Tax Compliance Services Providers:

Vertex, Inc. (www.vertexinc.com)

Legal Sources:

Martindale Hubble (https://martindale.com)
Contino + Partners (https://continopartners.com)

Equipment Lease Agreement

Agreement no.:	Purchase Option*: $___	Rent*: $___ in [advance] [arrears]	Advance Payment*: $___
Customer:	Total Financed Cost*: $___	No. Rent Payments:	No. Advance Payments: ___
DBA (if any):	Equipment Cost*: $___	Rent Period: Monthly	Description: 1st and Last
Address Line 1:	Soft Cost*: $___	Initial Term: ___ months	Documentation Fee*: $___
Address Line 2:	Financed Tax and fees: $___		Security Deposit: $
Address Line 3:	Equipment Description:	Soft Cost Description:	Equipment Location:
Phone: Fax:	See Exhibit A	See Exhibit A	See Exhibit A
Contact e-mail:			
Billing Address:	Billing e-mail:		*plus tax

This Lease Agreement ("Lease") contains the terms of your agreement with us. Please read it carefully. The words you, your, and Lessee mean you, our customer. The words we, us, our, and Lessor, mean ABC Leasing LLC.

1. EQUIPMENT; TERM AND ACCEPTANCE: We agree to lease to you and you agree to lease from us the equipment ("Equipment") described above, the cost of which shall include any services, software, installation and other items shown above ("Soft Costs"). The Equipment and Soft Costs items are together referred to as "Financed Items." You certify that the Financed Items will be used for business purposes, and not for personal, family, or household purposes. You will arrange for the delivery of the Equipment and Soft Cost items. No manufacturer, supplier, or salesperson is our agent, and their statements do not affect your rights or obligations under this Lease. You will promptly accept or reject the Financed Items upon delivery and, if accepted, you will promptly deliver a signed Acceptance Certificate in a form we provide. This Lease starts on the date that any of the Financed Items are accepted by you ("Commencement Date") and continues for the Interim Rent period (defined below) and the "Initial Lease Term" above. YOU AGREE THAT: THIS LEASE IS A NET LEASE AND MAY NOT BE TERMINATED OR CANCELED; YOU HAVE AN UNCONDITIONAL OBLIGATION TO MAKE ALL PAYMENTS DUE UNDER THIS LEASE ACCORDING TO THE TERMS SET FORTH HEREIN; AND YOU CANNOT WITHHOLD, SET OFF, ABATE, DEFER, OR REDUCE SUCH PAYMENTS FOR ANY REASON WHATSOEVER. If you signed a purchase agreement for the Financed Items, you hereby assign us the right, but not the obligation, to pay for the Financed Items and take title to the Equipment for the purposes of this Lease.

2. RENT AND FEES: You authorize us to adjust the Rent by not more than 20% if the actual Total Financed Cost differs from the estimated amount. You will pay the Rent and Tax in immediately available U.S. funds starting on the 1st day of the month immediately following the Commencement Date (but if the Commencement

Date is the 1st day of a month, the start date will be the Commencement Date) ("First Payment Date") and on the 1st day of each Rent Period during the term of the Lease until paid in full, adjusted for Advance Payments received. You will pay us "Interim Rent" for each day between the Commencement Date and the First Payment Date, calculated by dividing the Rent by the days in the Rent Period. You will pay the Documentation Fee, the Advance Payment, and the Security Deposit when you sign this Lease and a $175 administration fee at Lease end to cover our termination costs, which will be waived if you purchase the Equipment. At our request, you will make all payments by ACH.

3. ASSIGNMENT: YOU MAY NOT SELL, PLEDGE, TRANSFER, ASSIGN, OR SUBLEASE THE FINANCED ITEMS OR THIS LEASE. We may sell, assign, or transfer to any third party(ies) ("Assignee") all or any part of our interest in this Lease and/or the Financed Items without notice or consent. The Assignee (and its assigns) will have our rights, but none of our obligations. You may not assert against any assignee any claims, recoupment rights, defenses, or set-offs that you may have against us and/or any supplier or other person.

4. NO WARRANTIES: We are leasing the Equipment and financing the other Financed Items "AS-IS," "WHERE IS." YOU ACKNOWLEDGE THAT WE DO NOT MANUFACTURE THE EQUIPMENT OR PROVIDE ANY SOFT COST ITEMS; WE DO NOT REPRESENT ANY MANUFACTURER, DEVELOPER, OR SUPPLIER OF ANY EQUIPMENT OR SOFT COST ITEM, AND YOU SELECTED THE FINANCED ITEMS, MANUFACTURERS, AND SUPPLIERS IN YOUR OWN JUDGMENT. WE MAKE NO WARRANTIES, EXPRESS OR IMPLIED, INCLUDING WARRANTIES OF MERCHANTABILITY OR FITNESS, FOR PARTICULAR PURPOSE OR OTHERWISE. WE SHALL HAVE NO LIABILITY FOR ANY DAMAGES, WHETHER DIRECT, INDIRECT, GENERAL, SPECIAL, INCIDENTAL, EXEMPLARY, OR CONSEQUENTIAL, SUFFERED BY ANYONE IN CONNECTION WITH THE FINANCED ITEMS OR THIS LEASE. YOU AGREE YOU HAVE NOT RELIED ON US OR OUR REPRESENTATIVES FOR ANY TAX OR ACCOUNTING ADVICE. We transfer to you for the term of this Lease our rights under the manufacturer and supplier warranties.

5. LOCATION, USE, REPAIR, AND RETURN: You agree to keep the Financed Items free from liens, claims, and encumbrances other than ours. You will keep and use the Financed Items only at the address set forth herein. You may not move the Financed Items without our prior written consent. At your own cost, you will keep the Equipment eligible for all manufacturer certifications, in compliance with all applicable laws, and in as good condition as when you received it, except ordinary wear and tear. You will not make any alteration, addition, or replacement to the Equipment without our prior written consent. All alterations, additions, and replacements will become our property at no cost to us. We may inspect the Equipment during normal business hours. Unless you purchase the Equipment at the end of this Lease, you will immediately deliver the Equipment and other Financed Items, as applicable, to the location directed by us in the above-described condition, with all stored data and third-party software removed.

ACCEPTANCE	THIS LEASE MAY NOT BE CANCELED

(Lessee)	ABC Leasing LLC
By: X_____	By: X_____
Authorized Signer Title	Authorized Signer Title
Print Name_____ Date	Print Name_____ Date
Address:_____	Address:_____

Personal guaranty

When we use the words you and your in this Guaranty, we mean the Guarantor(s) indicated below. When we use the words we, us, our, and Lessor in this Guaranty, we mean ABC Leasing LLC. All other terms have the meanings used in this Lease. You guaranty that Lessee will make all payments and perform all other obligations under this Lease, and that this Lease may be modified by Lessee and us without notice or consent to you. Your obligations are continuing, direct, and unconditional. You waive notice of Lessee's default, acceptance, demand, and protest. You may not assign this Guaranty. This Guaranty is binding upon your permitted successors and assigns and inures to the benefit of our successors and assigns. If there is more than one Guarantor, your obligations are joint and several. You retroactively and prospectively authorize us and our affiliates to obtain credit bureau reports regarding your credit and make other credit inquiries in our discretion. We may simultaneously pursue you and Lessee to recover amounts due under this Lease. You are responsible for any and all legal fees and/or court costs incurred in relation to or connection with this Guaranty. THIS GUARANTY IS GOVERNED BY THE LAWS OF NEW YORK OR. YOU CONSENT TO THE JURISDICTION OF ANY COURT LOCATED WITHIN NEW YORK OR, IF APPLICABLE, THE ASSIGNEE JURISDICTION. YOU AND WE EXPRESSLY WAIVE ANY RIGHT TO A TRIAL BY JURY.

(Guarantor)	(Guarantor)
Guarantor: X _____	Guarantor: X_____
Print Name: _____ Date_____	Print Name:_____ Date:_____

You will pay all shipping and other expenses, and you will insure the Financed Items for full replacement value during shipping. You will maintain and operate the Financed Items in compliance with all applicable laws and regulations.

6. TAX: You agree to pay when due or reimburse us for all taxes, fines, and penalties (collectively, "Tax") relating to the Soft Costs items, the Equipment or this Lease, now or hereafter imposed or assessed. At our discretion, we will file and remit all sales, use, and personal property tax and you agree to pay estimated property taxes as invoiced by us our reasonable administrative fees. We do not have to contest any Tax.

7. CASUALTY AND INSURANCE: You will install and keep the Financed Items in good working order. Except for ordinary wear and tear, you are responsible for protecting the Financed Items from damage and loss of any kind. If the Financed Items are damaged or lost, you will continue to pay the amounts due and to become due hereunder without setoff or defense. During the term, you will (a) insure the Financed Items against all loss or damage for full replacement value naming us as sole lender loss payee; (b) obtain third-party general liability insurance (covering death and personal injury) with a minimum limit of $1 million combined single limit per occurrence (or such other amount as we

reasonably request) and third-party property damage insurance, naming us as an additional insured; and (c) deliver satisfactory evidence of such coverage with carriers, policy forms, and amounts acceptable to us. All policies must provide that we be given 30 days written notice of any material change or cancelation. If you do not provide evidence of acceptable insurance, we have the right, but no obligation, to obtain insurance covering our interest in the Financed Items for the term and any renewals and, if we do, you will pay us as invoiced for the insurance premium and an administrative fee, upon which we may make a profit. Insurance we obtain will not insure you against third-party claims and may be canceled by us at any time. You will cooperate with us, our insurer and our agent in the placement of coverage and with claims. If you provide evidence of acceptable insurance, we will cancel the insurance we obtained. Upon any loss or damage to any Financed Item, you will promptly notify us and, with our consent (not unreasonably withheld), promptly either repair or replace the Financed Items with comparable items satisfactory to us, provided that upon loss or damage beyond repair we may require you to pay us the amounts due under Section 9(ii) less any proceeds we receive from the insurance described herein. You authorize us to sign on your behalf and appoint us as your attorney-in-fact to endorse in your name any insurance drafts or checks issued due to loss or damage to any Financed Items. NOTHING IN THIS SECTION RELIEVES YOU OF RESPONSIBILITY FOR INSURANCE COVERAGE OR PAYMENTS UNDER THIS LEASE.

8 LATE CHARGES; DEPOSIT; SECURITY INTEREST AND FINANCIAL INFORMATION: If any Rent or other payment amount is not made when due, you agree to pay a late charge at the rate of ten percent (10%) of such late payment; and, for each Rent thereafter (or as otherwise invoiced by us), you agree to pay a finance charge of one and one-half percent (1.5%) per month on any unpaid delinquent balance, not to exceed the maximum rate allowable under applicable law. Any Security Deposit under this Lease will, at the end of this Lease, either be returned to you without interest (unless otherwise required by law) or used to offset any unpaid charges, provided that all of your Lease obligations have been met. Unless your purchase option is $1 or an Obligated Purchase is indicated above ("Obligated Purchase Lease"), we retain title to the Equipment. You hereby grant us a conditional security interest in the Financed Items (including any replacements, substitutions, additions, and attachments) and all proceeds thereof to secure your obligations under this Lease in the event this transaction is deemed a sale. You agree the Equipment is personal property, regardless of the manner of installation and you authorize us to file financing statements. Upon request, you will promptly provide us with financial information we deem reasonably necessary to determine your financial condition, including tax returns and compiled, reviewed, or audited financial statements.

9. DEFAULT; REMEDIES: Each of the following is a "Default" under this Lease: (a) you fail to pay any Rent or other amount within 5 days of its due date or you or any guarantor makes any false statement or misrepresentation to us; (b) you fail to perform any of your other obligations under this Lease or any other agreement with us or with any of our affiliates, and this failure continues for 10 days after notice; (c) you die, become insolvent, dissolve or are dissolved, fail to pay your debts as they mature, suffer a material adverse change in financial, business, or operating condition, assign your assets for the benefit of creditors, or voluntarily or involuntarily enter any bankruptcy or reorganization proceeding; (d) any guarantor of this Lease dies, does not perform its obligations under, or repudiates the guaranty, or becomes subject to one of the events listed above; or (e) you or any guarantor transfers substantially all of your/its assets or transfers a controlling interest in your/its ownership to any third party without our prior written consent. If

a Default occurs, we may do one or more of the following: (i) cancel or terminate this Lease and/or any or all other agreements that we have entered into with you; (ii) require you to immediately pay us, as compensation for loss of our bargain and not as a penalty, a sum equal to (A) all unpaid amounts then due under this Lease plus, (B) all unpaid Rent for the remainder of the Initial Term plus our anticipated end-of-lease (residual) interest in the Financed Items, each discounted, as of the date of payment, to present value at the rate of 2% per annum, which amount you agree is a reasonable estimation of our damages; (iii) require you to deliver the Financed Items to us as set forth in Section 5; (iv) repossess the Financed Items without court order, in which case, you will not make any claims against us for damages or trespass or any other reason; and/or (v) exercise any other right or remedy available at law or in equity. You agree to pay all of our costs of enforcing our rights against you, including reasonable attorneys' fees and costs. If we repossess Financed Items, we may sell or otherwise dispose of them without notice at a public or private sale and apply the net proceeds (after we have deducted all related costs) to amounts that you owe us. You will remain responsible for any balance due. Our remedies are cumulative, are in addition to any other provided for by law, and may be exercised concurrently or separately. Failure or delay by us to exercise any right shall not operate as a waiver of any right or modify the terms hereof.

10. FINANCE LEASE: If Article 2A-Leases of the Uniform Commercial Code applies, this Lease is a "finance lease" as defined therein. You acknowledge that (a) you have reviewed, approved, and received, a copy of the purchase agreements for the Financed Items or (b) we have informed you of the identity of the applicable manufacturers and suppliers, that you may have rights under such agreements, and that you may contact them for a description of those rights. TO THE EXTENT PERMITTED BY LAW, YOU WAIVE ANY AND ALL RIGHTS AND REMEDIES CONFERRED UPON A LESSEE BY ARTICLE 2A (508–522).

11. LEASE END OPTIONS; RENEWAL: At the end of the Initial Term, if no Default exists you may purchase all (but not less than all) of the Financed Items owned by us at the Purchase Option, plus Tax. Unless the purchase option price is $1.00 or this is an Obligated Purchase Lease, you must give us at least 60-day notice before the end of the Initial Term that you will purchase the Financed Items or that you will return the Financed Items to us. If you do not give us timely written notice or if you do not purchase or deliver the Financed Items to us in accordance with this Lease, this Lease will automatically renew for successive 1-month terms until you give us notice as stated above or we give you notice. During any such renewal terms, the Rent will remain the same. If you have a Fair Market Value ("FMV") Purchase Option, we will use our reasonable judgment to determine the Financed Items fair market value, which will be determined on an in-place value. Upon payment of the purchase price, we will transfer our interest in the Equipment to you "AS IS, WHERE IS" without any representation or warranty whatsoever and this Lease will terminate.

12. INDEMNIFICATION: You are responsible for and will indemnify and hold us harmless from any (a) losses, damages, penalties, claims, suits, and actions (collectively "Claims") caused by or related to the manufacture, installation, ownership, use, lease, financing, possession, or delivery of the Financed Items and/or any defects in, or inadequate or non-performance of, the Financed Items, and (b) all costs and attorneys' fees incurred by us relating to any Claim. You will reimburse us for and, if we request, defend us with attorneys we reasonably approve, at your cost and expense, against any Claims. This Section 12 survives termination of this Lease.

13. FAX/ELECTRONIC EXECUTION: A fax or electronically transmitted version of this Lease when received by us shall be binding on you for all purposes as if originally signed and the only version of the

Lease that is the original for all purposes is the version containing your original, fax or electronically transmitted signature and our original signature. If you elect to sign and transmit a Lease by fax or electronically by email, you waive notice of our acceptance and receipt of a copy of the originally signed Lease. This Lease becomes binding on us when executed by us and we may cancel this Lease if receipt of the Acceptance Certificate is delayed. The definitive version of this Lease is the document we delivered to you, which may not be modified without our consent.

14. MISCELLANEOUS: (a) Unconditional Payment. YOU ACKNOWLEDGE THAT YOUR OBLIGATIONS UNDER THIS LEASE, INCLUDING, BUT NOT LIMITED TO, YOUR UNCONDITIONAL OBLIGATION TO MAKE ALL PAYMENTS TO US, ARE ABSOLUTE AND UNCONDITIONAL AND SHALL BE MADE TO US WITHOUT DEFENSE, ABATEMENT, WITHHOLDING, CLAIM, COUNTERCLAIM, SET-OFF, OR REDUCTION FOR ANY REASON AND WILL IN NO MANNER BE AFFECTED BY ANY OTHER AGREEMENT YOU MAY HAVE WITH US OR ANY OTHER PERSON AND/OR THE PERFORMANCE, USEFULNESS, OR VALUE OF THE FINANCED ITEMS. (b) Choice of Law. This Lease shall be governed by the laws of New York, without regard to conflict of laws principles. (c) Jurisdiction. YOU CONSENT TO THE JURISDICTION OF ANY LOCAL, STATE, OR FEDERAL COURT LOCATED IN NEW YORK, OR, IF SOLD, ASSIGNED OR TRANSFERRED, THE ASSIGNEE'S JURISDICTION OF ORGANIZATION, OR ITS PRINCIPAL PLACE OF BUSINESS, AS ELECTED BY ASSIGNEE. (d) Jury Trial. YOU AND WE EXPRESSLY WAIVE TRIAL BY JURY AS TO ALL ISSUES ARISING OUT OF OR RELATED TO THIS LEASE. (e) Entire Agreement. This Lease constitutes the entire agreement between you and us and supersedes all prior agreements and understandings with respect to the subject matter hereof. (f) Enforceability. If any provision of this Lease is unenforceable, illegal, or invalid, the remaining provisions shall continue to be effective. (g) Amendment. This Lease may not be modified or amended except by a writing signed by you and us. You agree however, that we are authorized, without notice to you, to supply missing information or correct obvious errors in the Lease. (h) Notice. All notices shall be in writing and shall be delivered to the appropriate party personally by facsimile or by private courier, or by mail, postage prepaid, at its address (or phone number) shown herein or to such other address (or phone number) as directed in writing by such party reasonably in advance. (i) Usury. It is the express intent of both of us not to violate any applicable usury laws or to exceed the maximum interest rate permitted by applicable law, any excess payment to be applied to the Lease payments in inverse order of maturity with any remaining excess to be refunded to you. (j) Prepayment. Prepayment or early termination of this Lease is not permitted, except as we may permit. (k) Purchase Order. If a purchase order or other purchase agreement is attached to this Lease, it is solely for the purposes of identifying the Financed Items, and none of the terms or conditions thereof shall be deemed part of this Lease or to modify this Lease in any manner. (l) Assurances. You will promptly execute and deliver such other documents, as we reasonably request to protect our interests hereunder and carry out the intent of this Lease. (m) E-billing. We reserve the right to charge processing fee for paper invoicing and termination of the ACH payment.

Proposal Stage Checklist

The following checklist is a guide to identifying financing issues and in preparing and negotiating an equipment financing proposal. If other products are involved, such as software or services, they should similarly be addressed.

- **The Basic Financing Offer**
  - A lease
  - A conditional sale
  - A managed services arrangement
  - A fee-per-use agreement
  - Other
- **The Lessee or Obligor**
  - Has the lessee or obligor been accurately identified?
- **The Equipment Description**
  - What type will be involved?
  - Has the manufacturer of all the equipment been stated?
  - What is the model for each item of equipment?
  - How many units will be involved?
- **The Equipment Cost**
  - What is the total cost involved, both hard costs and soft costs, such as installation costs?
  - What is the cost per item?
  - Is the cost per item fixed?
    (1) If not, what is the likely cost escalation?
- **The Equipment Delivery**
  - What is the anticipated equipment delivery date?
    (1) What terms, if any, will change if the product delivery date is passed?
- **The Equipment Location**
  - Where will the equipment be located?
    (1) At the financing inception?
    (2) During the financing term?

- **The Financing Payments**
  - What is the primary financing payment structure?
    (1) When will the first payment be due?
    (2) Will the payments be payable in advance or in arrears?
    (3) Will the payments be due annually, semi-annually, quarterly, monthly, or other?
    (4) Will there be an interim financing payment payable (such as rent for the period prior to the start of any primary, or main, lease term) if the primary financing term does not to start on equipment delivery and acceptance under the financing contract? If so, how will it be computed, such as based on a daily equivalent of the primary rent?
- **The Term of the Financing**
  - How long will the financing term run?
    (1) Primary financing term
    (2) Renewal period
  - Will an interim financing term be involved? If so,
    (1) When will the interim term start?
    (2) When will the primary term start?
- **Options**
  - What special rights will the customer be offered, if any?
    (1) Fixed price purchase right
    (2) Fair market value purchase right
    (3) Fixed price renewal right
    (4) Fair market rental value renewal right
    (5) Right of first refusal
    (6) Termination right
    (7) Upgrade right
    (8) Other
  - What special rights, if any, will the financing party have?
    (1) Fixed price sale right, often referred to as a put
    (2) Fixed price renewal right
    (3) Termination right
    (4) Other

- **Tax Aspects**
  - What tax assumptions in the case of a lease, if any, will the lessee have to indemnify the lessor for in the event of tax loss or inability to claim?
  - If there are lessee tax indemnifications, what events that result in tax benefit unavailability will trigger an indemnification payment?
    (1) Any reason
    (2) Acts or omissions of lessee
    (3) Acts or omissions of lessor
    (4) Change in law
- **Conditions**
  - What conditions must be satisfied before the lessor is committed?
    (1) Governmental or regulatory approvals
    (2) Licenses or authorizations
    (3) Favorable opinions of counsel
    (4) Maintenance or achievement of certain financial tests
    (5) Satisfactory audited financial statements
    (6) Acceptable documentation
    (7) Approval by the financing party's credit committee
    (9) Other
- **Submission and Award Dates**
  - When is the latest date on which the proposal can be accepted?

Checklist for Drafting and Negotiating a Lease Agreement

In preparing a well-drafted lease agreement, the parties should cover all the important issues involved in a transaction. The following checklist pinpoints the issues that should typically be addressed:

- **What form of lease is appropriate?**
  - A single transaction lease agreement
  - A master lease agreement
- **Does the lease agreement cover the following issues?**
  - Has a page index of all topic headings been included?
  - Have the parties been properly identified?
  - (1) Lessor
  - (2) Lesser
- **Is the lessee a valid legal entity?**
- **Has a factual summary of the circumstances giving rise to the transaction been included?**
- **Has the consideration for the transaction been stated?**
- **Have the key terms been defined in the definition section? For example:**
  - Affiliate
  - Business day
  - Buyer-furnished equipment
  - Equipment delivery date
  - Equipment manufacturer
  - Event of default
  - Event of loss
  - Fair market value
  - Interim rent
  - Lease
  - Lease period
  - Lease supplement
  - Lessor's cost
  - Lien
  - Overdue interest rate

- ◦ Primary rent
- ◦ Casualty loss value
- **If equipment will be delivered after the lease is signed, has a procedure for adding it been established?**
  - ◦ Can the lessee decide not to lease future-delivered equipment when it arrives? If so, will the lessee be obligated to pay:
    - (1) A non-utilization fee?
    - (2) A commitment fee?
  - ◦ Can future-delivered equipment be accepted for lease as it arrives, or must the lessee aggregate a minimum dollar amount?
- **The lease period should be defined**
  - ◦ Will there be an interim lease term? If so, when will it begin and end?
  - ◦ When will the primary term begin?
  - ◦ How long will the primary term run?
  - ◦ Will the lessee be permitted to renew the lease? If so, what is the renewal period arrangement?
- **The rent structure must be defined**
  - ◦ Will a percentage rent factor be used? If so, what may be included in the equipment cost base?
    - (1) Sales tax
    - (2) Transportation charges
    - (3) Installation charges
    - (4) Other
  - ◦ How much rent must be paid?
  - ◦ When will the rent be due?
  - ◦ How must the rent be paid?
    - (1) Check
    - (2) Wire transfer
    - (3) Other
  - ◦ Where must the rent be paid?
    - (1) Has a post office box or other address been specified?

- **Can or must the lessor adjust the rent charge if there is a tax law change affecting, favorably or unfavorably, the lessor's economic return?**
  - If a rent adjustment is provided for, has the exact criterion for making it been clearly specified?
  - If the tax law change applies to future-delivered equipment and a rent adjustment is not acceptable, can the party adversely affected elect to exclude the equipment?
- **Will the rent obligation be a hell or high-water obligation?**
- **What is the lessor's total dollar equipment cost commitment?**
  - Will a percentage variance be permitted?
- **Will the lessee be required to submit reports? For example:**
  - Financial reports
    (1) Profit and loss statements
    (2) Balance sheets
    (3) Other
  - Accident reports
    (1) Has a minimum estimated accident dollar amount been agreed upon below which a report is not required?
    (2) Will the lessee be obligated to immediately telephone if an accident occurs?
    (3) Lease conformity reports
    (4) Equipment location reports
    (5) Third-party claim reports
- **Has a time been established for when lessee reports are due?**
- **Has a general lessee reporting requirement been imposed as to reports that may be deemed necessary by the lessor in the future?**
- **Equipment maintenance**
  - Who has the responsibility for insuring proper maintenance?
    (1) Lessor
    (2) Lessee
    (3) A third party

- Who must bear the cost of the maintenance?
  - (1) Lessor
  - (2) Lessee
- Will maintenance records be required?
- Will the lessor be permitted access to the maintenance records?
  - (1) If so, at what times:
  - (2) Normal business hours
  - (3) Any time requested
- **Will equipment alterations be permitted? If so,**
  - Will the lessor's consent be required before:
    - (1) An addition that may impair the equipment's originally intended function or that cannot be removed without so impairing such function?
    - (2) Any change?
  - Who will have title to any addition or other alteration?
    - (1) If it can be easily removed without equipment damage?
    - (2) If it cannot be removed without function impairment?
  - What rights will the lessor have to buy the alteration?
- **Will certain lessor ownership protection filings be advisable or necessary?**
  - Federal regulatory agencies, such as the Federal Aviation Administration
  - Uniform Commercial Code
  - Other
- **If lessor ownership protection filings will be made, who has the responsibility for making them, and who must bear the expense?**
  - Lessor
  - Lessee
- **If the lessee must make the required filings for the lessor, will the lessee have to confirm they have been made?**
- **Will the equipment be marked with the lessor's name and address? If so, who will have the marking responsibility and expense?**

- ◦ Lessor
- ◦ Lessee
- **Has the lessee been specifically prohibited from using, operating, storing, or maintaining the equipment carelessly, improperly, in violating the law, or in a manner not contemplated by the manufacturer?**
  - ◦ If the lessee must use the equipment for a purpose other than intended, has an exception been negotiated?
- **The lessee must be required to provide certain key representations**
  - ◦ That the lessee is properly organized, validly existing, and in good standing
  - ◦ That it has proper authorization to do business in the state where the equipment will be located
  - ◦ That the lessee has the transactional authority to enter into the lease
    - (1) That necessary board of director approvals have been obtained covering the transaction *and* the person signing the lease on behalf of the lessee
    - (2) That any other required approvals have been obtained
  - ◦ That there are not conflicting agreements
    - (1) Bank credit agreements
    - (2) Other loan agreements
    - (3) Mortgages
    - (4) Other leases
  - ◦ That all necessary regulatory approvals have been obtained
  - ◦ That there are no pending or threatened adverse legal or administrative proceedings that would affect the lessee's operations or financial condition
  - ◦ That there have been no adverse changes as of the lease closing in the lessee's financial condition since the latest available financial statements
- **The lessor must be required to provide certain key representations**

- ○ That the lessor has the transactional authority to lease the equipment
- ○ That any necessary board of director approval has been obtained
- ○ That any other approvals have been obtained or, if none is required, a statement that none is required
- ○ That the lessor will pay for the equipment in full
- ○ That the lessor will not interfere with the lessee's use of the equipment
  - (1) Has an exception when the lessee is in default been negotiated by the lessor?
- **The lessee should require product warranties to be assigned if the lessor has no equipment defect responsibility**
  - ○ If the warranties are not assignable, the lessor should be required to act on the lessee's behalf
- **Who has the responsibility for equipment casualty losses?**
  - ○ Lessor
  - ○ Lessee
- **Do the casualty loss values give adequate financial protection to the lessor?**
- **Are the casualty loss values competitive from the lessee's viewpoint?**
- **As of what time will a casualty loss be deemed to have occurred and has a *loss date* been defined?**
  - ○ What obligations change or come into effect on the loss date?
- **When is the casualty loss value payable, and when does interest on the amount payable begin to run?**
- **What taxes must be paid?**
  - ○ Sales tax
  - ○ Property taxes
  - ○ Rental taxes
  - ○ Withholding taxes
  - ○ Income taxes
  - ○ Other

- **Who must pay the taxes?**
  - The lessor
  - The lessee
- **For any taxes that a lessee must reimburse a lessor for payment, does the lessee have the right to have the taxes contested?**
  - What happens if the lessor does not fully pursue their contest remedies?
- **Is each party required to immediately notify the other of any tax imposition for which they will be responsible?**
- **Do the parties intend a true tax lease? If so,**
  - Inconsistent actions and filings should be prohibited
  - Will tax loss indemnifications be required?
  - Will any tax indemnity cover all lessor tax losses or only those resulting from the lessee's acts or omissions?
- **Who has the economic risk of a change in tax law?**
  - For past-delivered equipment
  - For future-delivered equipment
    - (1) Can either party elect not to lease if the economics are no longer favorable?
- **Has a formula been agreed on for measuring the amount of any tax benefit loss and the amount of any required reimbursement?**
  - Does the formula make the indemnified party whole?
- **Has the tax loss date been determined?**
- **Who has the expense responsibility for the equipment return, and where must it be returned to:**
  - If the lease ends normally?
  - If the lease ends prematurely?
- **May either party designate an alternative return location? If so, what is the expense responsibility?**
- **The lessor should be able to terminate the lease early or take other protective action in certain situations**
  - When the rent is not paid
  - When the lessee makes an unauthorized transfer of the equipment or any of its rights under the lease

- When there is a general failure to perform the obligations under the lease
- When the lessor discovers the lessee has made a material misrepresentation
- When there is a bankruptcy or similar event that would jeopardize the lessor's position

- **What actions can the lessor take in the event of default?**
  - Court action
  - Terminate the lease
  - Cause a redelivery of the equipment
  - Cause the lessee to store the equipment
  - Sell the equipment under its own terms
  - Be able to hold or re-lease the equipment
  - Be entitled to a predetermined amount of money as damages for a lease default

- **Certain lessor assignment rights may be desirable or required**
  - To a lender as security
  - To a purchaser

- **Will the lessee be able to sublease the equipment? If so,**
  - Will the lessee remain primarily liable under the lease during the sublease period?
  - Will the lessor have any control over who the sublessee will be?

- **Have all the lessor's options been included? For example:**
  - Right to terminate the lease
  - Right to force a sale of the lessee
  - Right to abandon the equipment
  - Right to force a lease renewal

- **Have all the lessee's options been included? For example:**
  (1) A purchase right, fixed or fair market value
  (2) A renewal right, fixed or fair rental value
  (3) A termination right
  (4) A right of first refusal
  (5) An upgrade financing right

- Will a defaulting lessee retain any of its option rights under the lease?
- Has the law of a jurisdiction been specified to control any issues that arise under the lease?
- Is there a severability clause?
- Is there any interest penalty for overdue payments?
- Has each side specified how and where any required notifications and payments will be made?
  - The address where notifications and payments must be sent
  - The way the notifications and payments must be made
    (1) U.S. mail
    (2) Other
- Has the signature section been set up properly for:
  - An individual
  - A corporation
  - A partnership
  - A trust
  - Other
- Has the signature been made in the proper capacity?

Supplemental Lease Document Closing Checklist

Although the type of additional closing documents required in a lease or other financing transaction will vary with each situation, the following checklist can be used as a general guideline, as applicable.

Legal Opinions:
- Is the lawyer rendering the legal opinion thoroughly experienced in the area to be covered by the opinion? For example, if an opinion is required on complex tax issues, is he or she fully knowledgeable on all the relevant aspects?
- How extensive are any legal opinion qualifications? That is, has the lawyer inserted so many conditions that he or she really has provided little comfort?
- To the extent that the legal opinion is based on facts supplied to the lawyer, are the facts accurate and complete?

Does the opinion of the lessee's or obligor's lawyer, to be delivered to the lessor or financing company, address the following issues?

- Proper organization, valid existence, and good standing of the lessee.
- The lessee's or obligor's full authority to enter into the lease or financing contract.
- The lessee's or obligor's complete and unrestricted ability to perform all obligations.
- Whether all the lessee's or obligor's lease commitments are legally binding.
- Whether all necessary consents have been obtained.
- Whether all necessary regulatory approvals have been obtained.
- Whether there are any pending or threatened adverse court or administrative proceedings. If so, what the potential impact may be.
- Whether any law, rule, or collateral agreement will be violated by the lessee or obligee entering the lease transaction.

Does the opinion of the lessor's or financing party's lawyer, to be delivered to the lessee or obligor, address the following issues?

- Whether the lessor or financing party is properly organized, validly existing, and in good standing.
- Whether the lessor or financing party is properly authorized to do business in the jurisdiction where the equipment will be located.
- Whether the transaction has been fully authorized by the lessor for financing party. For example, have all necessary committee and board of director or governing body approvals been secured?
- Whether all the lessor's or financing party's commitments are binding.
- Whether the lessor's or financing party's ability to perform its obligations is unrestricted.
- Whether any shareholder, lender, and so on consents are necessary. If so, have they been obtained?
- Whether the transaction will violate any law, rule, or collateral agreement as to the lessor or financing party.

Does the opinion of the lessor's or financing party's lawyer, to be delivered to any third-party lender, address the following issues?

- Whether the lessor or financing party is properly organized, validly existing, and in good standing.
- Whether all necessary authorizations, both as to the lease financing and any loan financing, have been obtained.
- Whether any loan obligations are fully enforceable against the lessor.
- Whether the lessor has good and marketable title to the leased equipment.
- Whether the equipment has any liens or encumbrances on it.
- Whether the lessor's rights under any lease are unencumbered, including their right to receive the rent payments.

Does the opinion of the guarantor's lawyer, to be delivered to the lessor or financing party, address the following issues?

- Whether the guarantor is properly organized, validly existing, and in good standing.
- Whether all necessary authorizations as to the lease or other financing have been obtained.
- Whether the lease or loan obligations are fully enforceable against the guarantor.

Does the opinion of the product vendor's lawyer, to be delivered to the lessor, address the following issues?

- Whether the title of the equipment will be delivered free and clear to the lessor.
- Whether all necessary internal authorizations have been obtained.

Has the lessor or financing party been supplied with the required obligor, obligor's controlling corporation, and any obligor's guarantor financial statements?

- Profit and loss statements.
- Balance sheets.
- Financial officer's certificate updating the prior financial statements to the closing.

Have adequate applicable financial statements or information been obtained?

- Profit and loss statements.
- Balance sheets.
- Financial officer's certificate updating the prior financial statements to the closing.

Have all the critical financial statements been certified by an independent certified public accounting firm?

Has a certified copy of any relevant corporate board of director resolutions or other governing authority been delivered?

If the lease or loan obligations will be guaranteed by a third party, will it be a full and unconditional guarantee? If not, is the limited extent of the guarantee understood?

If personal injury and property damage insurance is required, does the insurance company's certificate of insurance properly represent the required insurance?

If third-party equipment is involved, has the financing obligor entered into a purchase agreement with the third-party equipment supplier and has a purchase agreement assignment been provided?

- Does any equipment purchase agreement assignment specifically provide that only the rights, not the obligations, will be transferred to the lessor?
- Under an equipment purchase agreement assignment, will the lessor be entitled to all third-party vendor supplied services, training, information, warranties, and indemnities?
- Has the third-party equipment vendor's consent been obtained for the purchase agreement assignment? If so, does it (1) acknowledge the assignment and (2) acknowledge that the lessor will not have to buy the equipment if the lessee backs out before the lease is executed?

Has any necessary equipment bill of sale been included? If so,

- Is it a warranty bill of sale?
- Does it contain a representation that the seller has the lawful right and authority to sell the equipment?

If the equipment will be located on leased or mortgaged property, has the landowner or mortgagee supplied a written waiver of any present or future claim to the leased or financed equipment?

Have appropriate UCC financing statements (UCC-1s) been prepared for filing?

A Quick "True" Lease Checklist

The following checklist can be used as a guide to determine whether a lease transaction's basic features comply with the *guidelines'* requirements. If any answer is "No," there may be a problem.

	YES	NO
1. Has the lessor made an initial equity investment equal to at least 20 percent of the equipment cost?	[ ]	[ ]
2. Is the initial equity investment unconditional in nature?	[ ]	[ ]
3. Will the lessor's minimum investment remain equal at least to 20 percent of the equipment cost during the lease term?	[ ]	[ ]
4. Is the estimated residual value of the equipment at least equal to 20 percent of the equipment's original cost?	[ ]	[ ]
5. Will the useful life of the equipment remaining at the end of the lease term be equal to the longer of one year or 20 percent of the originally estimated useful life?	[ ]	[ ]
6. If there is a lessee purchase option, is it at fair market value as of the time of exercise?	[ ]	[ ]
7. Is the lessor without any rights to force a sale of the equipment to any party?	[ ]	[ ]
8. Is the lessor without any specific right to abandon the equipment?	[ ]	[ ]
9. Has the lessor furnished all the equipment cost other than any third-party debt?	[ ]	[ ]
10. Will the lessor have to bear the cost of any permanent equipment improvement, modification, or addition?	[ ]	[ ]
11. If the lessee pays for a severable improvement, could the equipment be used for its intended use without it?	[ ]	[ ]
12. If the lessee pays for a severable improvement, can the lessor buy it only at a price at least equal to its fair market value?	[ ]	[ ]
13. If the lessee pays for a non-severable improvement, could the equipment be used for its intended use without the improvement?	[ ]	[ ]
14. If the lessee pays for a non-severable improvement, will someone other than the lessee be able to use the equipment?	[ ]	[ ]
15. Does every non-severable improvement that is paid for by the lessee, not constitute a lessee investment?	[ ]	[ ]

16. Will the lessor pay for any equipment cost overruns?	[ ]	[ ]
17. Are all the equipment loans from lenders unrelated to the lessee?	[ ]	[ ]
18. Is the transaction devoid of any indebtedness guarantees by the lessee or related parties?	[ ]	[ ]
19. Will the lessor make a profit on the lease without considering the tax benefits?	[ ]	[ ]
20. Will the transaction generate a positive cash flow for the lessor?	[ ]	[ ]
21. Will the equipment have a use at the end of the lease term to someone other than to the lessee?	[ ]	[ ]
22. Have the required backup information and material been submitted with the request for ruling?	[ ]	[ ]

About the Author

Richard M. Contino, Esq., is an internationally recognized attorney, equipment leasing advisor, seminar instructor, and a businessman, experienced in the legal, business, marketing, and financial aspects of equipment financing. He is the Managing Director of First Lease Advisors, an equipment leasing and financing consulting firm; the Managing Director of Fairfield Capital Group, LLC, an equipment lease syndication firm; and the Managing Partner of Contino + Partners, a law firm whose practice is limited to equipment leasing and financing. He has an LLM (Corporate Law) from the New York University Graduate School of Law; a Juris Doctor from the University of Maryland School of Law and a Bachelor of Aeronautical Engineering from Rensselaer Polytechnic Institute. He is a member of the Bar of the State of New York and has been admitted to the Bars in the State of Maryland and the District of Columbia. Richard Contino is also a member of the American and New York State Bar Associations and is listed in Who's Who of American Law, Who's Who of Emerging Leaders, Who's Who in the World, and The International Who's Who of Contemporary Achievement. He is the author of the following books and book material:

- *COMMERCIAL LAW & PRACTICE GUIDE*, LexisNexis Matthew Bender, 2008, 2018 (Revision Leasing Editor)
- *New York Commercial Law (2012 Edition)*, LexisNexis Matthew Bender (UCC Art. 2A Chapter Author)
- *THE COMPLETE HANDBOOK OF EQUIPMENT LEASING*, AMACOM BOOKS 2002 and 2006; Second Edition, 2015
- *ASSET-BASED FINANCING*, LexisNexis Matthew Bender, 2006 (Revision Tax Editor)
- *THE COMPLETE BOOK OF EQUIPMENT LEASING AGREEMENTS*, AMACOM Books, 1997

- *HANDBOOK OF EQUIPMENT LEASING*, AMACOM Books, 1989; Second Edition, 1996
- *NEGOTIATING BUSINESS EQUIPMENT LEASES*, McGraw-Hill, 1995, Second Edition, 1998
- *LEGAL AND FINANCIAL ASPECTS OF EQUIPMENT LEASING TRANSACTIONS*, Prentice-Hall, 1979
- *THE FRANCHISING HANDBOOK*, AMACOM Books, 1993 (Finance Author)
- *TRUST YOUR GUT! - A Practical Guide to Developing and Using Intuition for Business*, AMACOM Books, 1996

Index

OTHER TITLES IN THE BUSINESS LAW AND CORPORATE RISK MANAGEMENT COLLECTION

John Wood, Econautics Sustainability Institute, Editor

- *Conversations in Cyberspace* by Giulio D'Agostino
- *Cybersecurity Law: Protect Yourself and Your Customers* by Shimon Brathwaite
- *Understanding Cyberrisks in IoT: When Smart Things Turn Against You* by Carolina A. Adaros Boye
- *How New Risk Management Helps Leaders Master Uncertainty* by Robert B. Pojasek
- *AI Concepts for Business Applications* by Nelson E. Brestoff

Announcing the Business Expert Press Digital Library

Concise e-books business students need for classroom and research

This book can also be purchased in an e-book collection by your library as

- a one-time purchase,
- that is owned forever,
- allows for simultaneous readers,
- has no restrictions on printing, and
- can be downloaded as PDFs from within the library community.

Our digital library collections are a great solution to beat the rising cost of textbooks. E-books can be loaded into their course management systems or onto students' e-book readers.
The **Business Expert Press** digital libraries are very affordable, with no obligation to buy in future years. For more information, please visit **www.businessexpertpress.com/librarians**. To set up a trial in the United States, please email **sales@businessexpertpress.com**.

www.ingramcontent.com/pod-product-compliance
Lightning Source LLC
Chambersburg PA
CBHW061212220326
41599CB00025B/4611